HE YOUNG CHILDREN
LEA ROUGH ACTIVITIES
n the early years

Hodder & Stoughton
A MEMBER OF THE HODDER HEADLINE GROUP

Orders: please contact Bookpoint Ltd, 78 Milton Park, Abingdon, Oxon OX14 4TD. Telephone: (44) 01235 827720, Fax: (44) 01235 400454. Lines are open from 9.00 – 6.00, Monday to Saturday, with a 24 hour message answering service. Email address: orders@bookpoint.co.uk

British Library Cataloguing in Publication Data
A catalogue record for this title is available from The British Library

ISBN 0 340 780533

First published 2001
Impression number   10 9 8 7 6 5 4 3 2 1
Year   2005 2004 2003 2002 2001

Copyright © 2001 Jane Cole, Sheilagh Clark, Sue Hirschheimer, Terrie Martyn and Joy Morrall

Cover photo by Simon Emery/Simon Emery Associates
Typeset by Wyvern 21 Ltd, Bristol
Printed in Italy for Hodder & Stoughton Educational, a division of Hodder Headline Plc, 338 Euston Road, London NW1 3BH.

Contents

Acknowledgements

We would like to thank the children, families and colleagues we have worked with over the years and from whom we have learnt so much.

We need to thank particularly the 1998 and 1999 intake at Tunstall Nursery School and their parents, the staff team, the families using our Family Room and those at the Holiday Club.

We hope all involved will be pleased with our book and feel it reflects our learning community.

How This Book is Organised

The adults are key to the success of providing first hand experiences. This involves a good knowledge through observation of the children, their stage of development and their interests. The experiences need to be carefully planned involving parents/carers and linking into the community. Health and safety and equality issues need to be considered to allow all children to fully benefit from the experiences.

Adults are equally central to building on the experiences by providing the resources to extend and consolidate the learning, and by developing interaction with the children and linking into their developing interests to take the work forwards.

In **Part 2** these aspects, together with learning opportunities and NVQ links, are provided separately either at the end of each activity or at the end of each chapter for ease of reference.

We are not providing a specific aim/outcome for each activity illustrated, but indicate in detail a range of learning opportunities that it offers to meet the varied needs of young children.

The photographs were taken in our nursery school for 3 and 4 year-olds. The ideas depicted can be easily adapted into other settings in this Foundation Phase of education as well as within home care settings.

In **Part 3** we look at interaction with babies and toddlers within our Family Room. Again these apply in all settings and homes.

Part 4 shows children up to 8 years old making use of the workshop activities in a Holiday Club. Their more mature skills and interests extend the processes and outcomes.

1

Planning for Learning

This is not a book about scrunkled tissue and templates. It is about promoting children's learning.

It is not a set of step-by-step recipes for activities that adults can provide for children, where each child can take home an identical picture or model. This book involves the leader, through its illustrations and bullet points, in ways to interest and engage young children in creative learning. We show a diverse range of accessible and affordable activities and suggest how adults can observe and intervene to support the learning. We have linked the learning opportunities to the six areas of the Early Learning Goals and shown the relevant National Vocational Qualification (NVQs) in Early Years Care and Education, and Playwork. It will be a useful resource for practitioners, students and be of interest to parents, carers and other supporting professionals.

The starting point for each activity is not the adult's idea of a finished product but what engages the children at their stage of development. It is not what they have made but how they made it that is important. It is the process that promotes learning and not the product.

The way children learn is not 'tidy'. They go from one thing to another making links with their previous experiences and this is reflected in their understanding of the activities they are engaged with. Their learning is holistic and involves all aspects of the individual child. These aspects include a sense of well being in all dimensions of their life; physical, emotional, social, linguistic and intellectual.

Children need to be able to learn by making 'mistakes' in a secure environment. We all learn more when things go 'wrong' and we manage to put them 'right' to our satisfaction. Skills such as cutting masking tape enables children to experiment and through trial and error learn the properties of the material. At an appropriate time adults can offer strategies such as sticking the end of the tape onto the table and pulling out a small amount at a time to cut. This offers a technique which allows the child still to be in control of the activity and enables them to achieve success. It is important to judge the right moment; intervene too early and the adult is taking control; intervene too late and the child has lost interest or become frustrated. It is about enabling but not taking over the activity. The child's image of themselves as a competent and successful learner must be the outcome of all activities.

The activities must be part of children's play, not separate 'work', and be based on their current interests. We believe that children should make their own choices from a carefully planned and resourced learning environment which encourages curiosity, experimentation and independence. How the learning environment is set out and how the resources are offered to children will have a major impact on how they feel about themselves and their learning. We offer a workshop approach where resources as set out in open baskets and boxes clearly labelled with pictures and print on low level shelves from which children can choose. Routines can be established which encourage children to sort and replace resources after using them or at the end of a session. This engages them in practical learning opportunities and fosters a sense of responsibility. The adult's role is to establish a warm and trusting relationship with the child and, through this and on-going observation, achieve a good understanding of their stage of development and learning needs. The activities provided, and the way they are supported, offer relevant learning opportunities and the adult intervention enables effective progress.

It is not our intentions that are the most important. As early years practitioners we should be looking at what the children are interested in, what their experience, knowledge and skills are as the basis for activities to promote learning. Care should be taken when interpreting the Early Learning Goals to ensure that children are allowed to learn freely and not overly directed into learning specific 'goals'. Too often we are in such a hurry to promote the curriculum that we are giving children answers to questions that they are not yet ready to ask.

Children tune into learning in different ways at different times and with varying emphases. Some do it intellectually and through language, some visually and with their other senses and some through interaction with others. They often use a mixture of all these aspects to various degrees. To help children access learning and achieve, sensitivity is a prime requirement from the adult. There is a need to strike a balance between adult led and child initiated activities. Children need time to explore materials initially before they can use them in a play sequence or symbolic way. They use the same materials in many creative ways and experience them through their senses. Using prior knowledge and experience they learn together with others.

Children need to be challenged, the activities exciting and dynamic. They should be demanding but still within the child's reach. 'What the child can do with help today he can do on his own tomorrow'. (Vygotsky, 1978). This can be seen so clearly with babies who are determined and persevere at mastering skills such as standing and walking. The supporting adult needs to keep a balance between enabling the process of learning to continue successfully and over protecting the baby. Children with additional needs will still require opportunities to choose and become competent learners. They may need some input in a more systematic and structured way.

Our activities use accessible materials and equipment which early years practitioners can easily provide, extend or adapt to make them relevant to the children they are working with. In each chapter there are details of health, safety and equality issues.

Activities cannot be seen or planned in isolation. The way all the adults who are involved with the children share their strategies and the child's responses is vital. This is not a one-way or single channelled process. A true sharing of practices and expertise is the most effective use of the resources around the child at home and in the early years setting.

The cycle of regular observation, assessment, planning and evaluation is essential. Practitioners need to develop expertise in this area in order to promote the

Lapping up learning
It was a rainy afternoon and the children were asked to play under the veranda in the garden. Jobi decided that he wanted to taste the rain and William joined him.

development and achievement of all the children actively learning in their settings. While this needs to be recorded to give evidence of the purpose of activities and to show how and when children are achieving, we are concerned that copious checklists and repetitive compartmentalising of subject areas are not the best ways. While there does need to be written evidence, we have found that the regular ongoing discussion about the provision and what the children are doing is the most effective way to promote achievement. All the adults are involved and develop a common, consistent way of working which values everyone's contributions. Sharing ways of working and the achievements of children with families is also very powerful. It is with this in mind that this book offers a visual approach, through photographs, key points and raising questions. The photographs illustrate the planning of the activities through the resources and how they are accessed by the children.

Sharing their family folders
At the home visit each family is given a folder and invited to document their child's baby and toddler years. They bring this when they start at school. The folders are all accessible to the children who frequently share them with each other, staff and visitors. Some families take them home during the year and add in activities they do together. Each child's key worker will review the folder frequently and ensure all children have a range of work in them. Children often choose to file pieces of work themselves. They are very proud of this record of achievement.

Parents are the first and continuing educators of their children. These initial secure and supportive relationships will enable children to form relationships with others in the wider community. Children cannot get involved in a meaningful way with any activities until they feel comfortable and confident in the early years setting. This can be achieved in a planned way through the allocation of key workers, home visits and welcoming adults into the setting in a variety of ways. The attitudes and values of all the adults need to be explicit, shared and reviewed. This rigorous dialogue supports a learning community. Adults need to show a genuine interest and respect for children's ideas, interests and involvement.

All children are unique individuals in terms of their gender, abilities, needs, culture, beliefs, attitudes, language, relationships and experiences. These need to be respected and built on by early years practitioners. By providing a welcoming, open, well planned environment all children should have the benefit of fully inclusive, stimulating early education.

Activities with young children should aim to:

- build on what children know and can do
- be provided in a comfortable and relaxed setting
- ensure all children and adults feel valued
- enable all children and adults to access the learning and achieve

- allow children to make choices
- encourage children to explore and experiment
- foster independence
- promote confidence and self-esteem
- provide challenge and excitement
- build on what engages and interests
- encourage children and adults to share the learning
- enable children to make relationships with peers and adults
- help children to work towards co-operation with others
- encourage listening and questionning
- support the expression of ideas, findings and feelings.

Adults also need to be active learners and this should be acknowledged in early years settings where everyone is part of a learning community. Respect for each other and valuing the process of learning underpins all the activities.

Adults and children learning together provides many opportunities for social interaction and the promotion of children's emotional development. Almost all activities for young children will develop their senses, language and physical skills. All come together as each child forms schemas and concepts in their minds.

Our overall aim is to share with you the underlying principles of early learning so that the provision and support you and the home give to our very young children is effective in promoting achievement and progress. Our key message is to use the children's needs and interests as the starting point for planning for them as independent learners.

Friends painting together
Amy, Jessica and Natalie are enjoying the experience of making one big painting together.

2

First Hand Experiences as Starting Points for Learning

A child's imagination is fuelled though first hand experiences, such as an everyday occurrence in the home or going to the local shops. However, it is important to remember that some children's experiences are limited and therefore it is vital that we provide a range of opportunities through our settings. This can be done in a variety of ways: through going out on visits to places of interest; visitors/performers bringing performances in with puppets, drama, movement or music; books, videos and television programmes. All these help to spark the initial interest that captivates the involvement and imagination of young children.

As part of the planning for children's learning, practitioners can take advantage of their locality. We have found that visits to places in our local streets and community have been very effective in providing the experiences which enable children to make links in their learning as they develop concepts and skills through their play and interaction.

We have chosen the following two examples of visits in our locality which stimulated a lot of learning in our nursery. The many first experiences which can be used are demonstrated in our diagram on page 7.

■ VISIT TO A LOCAL GARAGE

Two school staff , Sue and Catrina, went to visit Alcin at home before she started at the nursery. Sue was to be her keyworker and shared with Alcin a folder of photographs about activities at nursery. There was one of a visit by a group of children, parents and staff to the local garage and the role play car wash that they had made on return to school. Alcin was fascinated and almost her first words when entering the school were 'car wash?' Alcin enjoyed filling up the wheeled toys with the pretend petrol hose pipe in the nursery garden and talk about cars and garages

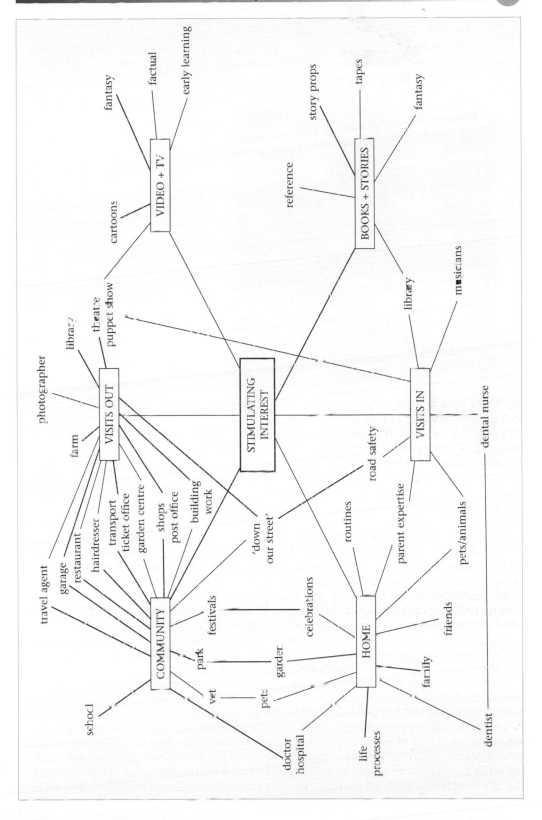

helped to extend her English vocabulary as her first language is Turkish. This fitted in well with the current theme of travel and transport to link with many children's experiences during the summer holidays, so staff planned a visit with a small group of children to the garage.

FIGURE 2.1   *Alcin pretends to fill up tricycle No. 4 with petrol from the hose. Hayley is paying her.*

A member of staff, Rukhsana, drove her people carrier around the corner to the garage while a group of children walked around with other staff and parent helpers. Some of the children decided which wash programme we needed and bought a ticket. Ten children and two adults fitted inside. Alcin's mum, Figen, put the ticket in the machine and Rukhsana drove through. The children experienced the car wash from inside the people carrier and were very excited to see the brushes go round and the water spraying.

Afterwards Rukhsana drove to the petrol pumps and the children watched the dials and numbers as she filled her tank. She counted out the money with the children and some went to help her pay. With one adult to two children everyone walked safely around the garage, the shop and adjoining car showrooms looking at the many interesting signs, brochures and objects.

On the walk back to nursery and at group time the children talked a lot about what they had seen and how they could set up a car wash at school. The children watched as staff printed out the digital stills photographs on the computer. The bag of garage resources was retrieved from the storage shed and the contents examined and discussed. Following this staff made the car washes basic structure and displayed photographs and other resource materials. Staff regularly visited the role play garage as customers and helped children develop and extend sequences of pretend play. Some children enjoyed using the tools, some re-enacted the washing and some played out the shop selling and taking orders on the telephone. Children became interested in the number plates and made them for the wheeled toys in the garden.

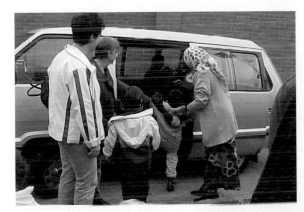

FIGURE 2.2　*Counting the children into the people carrier*

FIGURE 2.3　*Going through the car wash*

FIGURE 2.4　*Listening to the jets of water*

FIGURE 2.5   *Playing in the car wash role play at school*

FIGURE 2.6   *Looking at the photographs of the car wash*

Not all children in the class visited the garage on this occasion. Children who had shown interest in cars and transport were invited. The maturity of the children, a balance of boys and girls and the links with parents/carers were taken into account. Over time all children are given opportunities to go on trips and experience a wide range of first hand learning experiences. This stimulating visit enabled us to plan and develop further activities that made connections with this first hand experience. Many of these are illustrated throughout the book, e.g. forces/pushing/pulling/pipes and cars; musical scales/up and down the ladder; joining materials/can you make a ladder;singing '5 Jolly Firefighters'.

■ VISITING TRAMLINE BUILDING WORKS

The Tramlink system passes near the school and its construction was very interesting to local children and families. We took several groups of children with staff and parents to watch the work as it developed. As well as taking photographs to record what we saw the children made drawings and notes on clipboards. There was much discussion about safety issues and children entered a local competition for a poster to warn people of the dangers during construction.

FIGURE 2.7   *Watching the builders at work and all the machinery*

FIGURE 2.9   *Making notes of what they are looking at*

FIGURES 2.8, 2.10, 2.11, 2.12   *Daniel made drawings of the tram rails and chose to represent them in paint back at school. He described what he was representing: 'This is the tram line and the purple bits are to hold the lines down and then the nails are to hold the purple bits. You have to be careful when the tram comes.'*

FIGURES 2.13, 2.14, 2.15, 2.16
Watching the building work stimulated the children's interest and many extension activities developed from this. Many became engrossed in building with real bricks and play sand. The outside playhouse at the nursery became a builder's office with phones and order forms. After lots of experimenting and looking at patterns in walls some children started overlapping bricks. The interest was reinforced when we had a storage garage built in the garden.

■ PLANNING DIAGRAM FOR TRANSPORT THEME

Personal, Social and Emotional Development
Visit to local garage & carwash
Visit tramline building works
Sharing and co-operating
Awareness of safety/danger
Road Safety/Fire Drill

Communication, Language and Literacy
Recall and discussion about the trip
Print in the environment/road signs
Stories and reference books about transport
Writing signs in garage
Road Signs
Using prepositions

TRANSPORT

Knowledge and Understanding of the World
Links to types of transport
Can you make a car/bus/bike/ fire engine/tram?
Can you make a ladder/helmet?
Tyre rubbings
Awareness of local environment/maps/ journey to nursery
Knowledge of people's jobs
Hoses/water pressure/siphoning
Forces/pushing/pulling/pipes and cars
Joining materials

Mathematical Development
Number plates/recognition of numerals
Size of vehicles and wheels
Counting/matching/sorting cars
Using money/garage and role play
Measuring with trundle wheel

Creative Development
Garage role play/set up with children
Patterns with car tracks/wheels
Musical scales/up and down the ladder
Observational and representational drawings
Songs about transport/firefighters

Physical Development
Washing cars/bikes
Walking, stretching/crouching
Fine motor/joining materials
Gross motor/climbing ladders/ using hoses

Equal opportunities – access to the learning

- Boys and girls should be encouraged to participate in a variety of role play situations and avoid stereotypical roles.
- Role play areas and resources should be representative of a range of cultural experiences.
- Entrances to role play areas should be wide

enough to allow access for children with physical disabilities.

- Access arrangements and appropriate travel facilities should be checked for children with special needs.
- Venues of outings should be appropriate to the age/stage of the children.

Health and safety

- Correct ratio (as per registration/inspection) of adults to children must be adhered to on all visits and children constantly supervised. (It is best not to put name labels on young children as 'strangers' could then form a relationship if the children get separated. You may like to use a band or highly coloured hat/waistcoat so members of your group can be easily spotted. However, if each adult has two children, one in each hand, the danger of losing a child is minimal!)
- Vehicles should have seat belts and correct insurance.
- Children should hold adults or each other's hands.
- When exiting transport children should alight onto the pavement.
- Equipment should be kept clean and regularly checked for safety..
- Visitors should be carefully vetted and not be stereotypical.
- Dressing-up clothes should be fastened at the neck with velcro.
- The wearing of dressing-up clothes should be discouraged on any climbing equipment.
- Electrical equipment for use in play e.g. hairdrier, telephone, should have the flex removed.

Further reading, information and sources

Garnett, S. (1996) *The Home Corner*. Leamington Spa: Scholastic.

Henderson, A. (1991) *Make Believe*. Play Activity Series. Pre-school Learning Alliance.

NVQ links

Level 2

C 1.3, C 4.2, C 4.3, C 4.4, C 4.5, C 8.5, C 9.2, C 9.3, E 1.1, E 1.3, E 2.1, E 2.2, E 2.5, E 2.6, P 1.1

Level 3

C 3.3, C 3.4, C 5.2, C 5.3, C 5.4, C 5.5, C 7.2, C 10, C 11.2, C 11.3, C 11.4, C 11.5, C 15.1, C 15.2, C 15.4, E 3.1, E 3.3, M 7, P 2.3

THREE 3

Sensory Materials for Everyday Learning

Sensory engagement with materials around them enables babies and young children to explore and make sense of their world. At very early stages babies need to physically explore their the texture and properties of food although as they grow older it will be important to distinguish between food and play materials. It is essential to provide children with a range of safe materials which can be physically manipulated. This needs to be a process without an adult-prescribed end product thereby giving all children the confidence to gain skills and understand the materials they are using. Children will through this become excited and creative. They will spend long periods banging, moulding or squeezing the clay, dough or plasticine into many pleasing shapes. They will become confident to talk about what they have created expressing their own thoughts and feelings about what they are trying to achieve.

While children explore they are learning about textures and other attributes of the materials. The processes of squeezing, rolling and using small tools strengthens the muscles in their fingers and hands. This then helps their fine motor control and co-ordination and later skills such as pencil and mouse control.

Some children fear getting dirty and here the adult must be sensitive in persuading them to participate and eventually derive pleasure and satisfaction from handling mucky materials.

Children usually find modelling activities creative and therapeutic. Malleable materials can offer flexible opportunities for children with limited communications skills or who are needing to express feelings of sadness, loss or frustration.

■ PLAYDOUGH

A cheap malleable material. There are many recipes for cooked and uncooked dough. If you use just flour water and salt the dough can be baked, then painted and used as play material such as food in a shop/restaurant. Other types add oil to make it pliable and cream of tartar as a magic ingredient which brings it all together as you cook in a saucepan. The children can watch an adult making the dough and then handle when warm(need to make sure not too hot to handle!). This is one recipe we have used – it is good to experiment with quantities.

Ingredients: 3 large cups of cheapest plain flour; 1½ cups of cooking salt; 6 teaspoons of cream of tartar; 3 tablespoons of cooking oil; 3 cups of water.

Making: mix all the ingredients in a saucepan and cook over a low heat. The mixture will come together and come away from side of the pan. You may need to sprinkle flour on the table as children use if it is sticky.

Keep in a sealed container in a refrigerator. Keeps for quite a time depending on use.

WAYS OF PRESENTING AND USING

- add food colour (pastes create stronger colours), essences, glitter, sequins
- experiment with different flours and ingredients to alter the properties of the dough – involve the children
- put with – cooker and utensils
    cutters, moulds, rollers
    different tools such as potato mashers and garlic pressers to make marks/prints
    scissors and knives
    recyclable materials – empty containers from boxes of chocolates, egg boxes

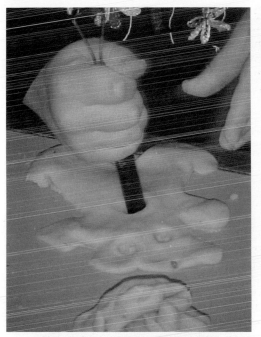

FIGURES 3.1, 3.2, 3.3 *Playdough cooking involving rolling, cutting, shaping, marking*

■ PLASTICINE

A variety of bought modelling materials are available. Some are very expensive and wonderfully soft. Cheaper varieties need warming before they become pliable. They need frequent replenishing as once colours are mixed all becomes a dull brown. With some varieties colours will blend.

WAYS OF PRESENTING AND USING

Similar to playdough and clay but particularly good for cutting skills. Exciting to model with especially as the children become more skilled in using it. Important to present attractively so that it is inviting to children.

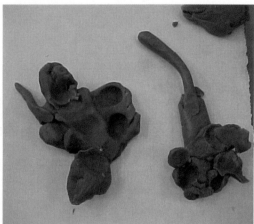

FIGURES 3.4, 3.5 *Rolling, cutting, shaping, pressing and modelling loads of lizards (Penny's current fascination) from the plasticine*

■ PAPER PULP

A cheap, recycled material. Satisfying individual and group activity to tear up the paper egg boxes and fun to add water. Needs many strong hands to squash and squeeze so that the material becomes pliable and can be shaped. Can only be kept wet for a limited period before decaying but can be moulded into shapes or pieces, dried out, painted and kept – will decay if gets damp again. Other sources of paper can be used but some are difficult to tear and some rather staining and unsuitable to use.

FIGURES 3.6, 3.7 *Tearing up egg boxes, adding water and working into a pulp (which can be mixed in a blender to make finer). You can use the pulp to model with or make a landscape for small world creatures to play in.*

■ CLAY

Relatively inexpensive to purchase and needs careful storing with wet cloths to keep from drying out. If kept well can be used over long periods. Satisfying material to handle and work with. Will dry hard enough to paint and keep for sometime. Some varieties will dry very hard without baking.

WAYS OF PRESENTING AND USING

- by itself on boards or floor tiles
- large shall trays as a group experience – add hand water sprayers to keep moist and change consistency
- use clay modelling tools
- printing with variety of items such as coins, bottle tops, lids
- mark making with materials as playdough
- mould around or inside different shaped containers
- making 3-dimensional models.

FIGURES 3.8, 3.9 *Squeezing, rolling, marking, hammering, cutting, smoothing the clay and making a face*

■ SAND

Relatively inexpensive material which is very versatile. Practitioners need to be sure that the sand they use is non staining and safe for children. Small bags of silver sand can be bought through catalogues and in toy shops but larger quantities can often be found in DIY supermarkets or garden centres. For our large outdoor pit we obtained jumping pit sand from a builders' merchant who delivered by the ton. Indoors sand should be open to the air or covered with fabric cloth.

Wet and dry sand have very different properties and it is important that children experience and experiment with these. Each setting needs to make their own arrangements to allow young children free and frequent access. It is important not to overcrowd the sand as the resources will influence the play. At times it may be useful to offer a restricted choice of resources, at other times access to a wide variety will allow children with different developmental needs to find satisfaction and will support progress in their learning. It is useful to vary the resources in the sand so that it gives the children fresh interest. Resources can be presented separately near by the sand for children to make choices.

WAYS OF PRESENTING AND USING

- present in a variety of containers such as shallow trays for concrete mixing, small individual trays, commercial sand trays for deeper digging
- a large outdoor sand pit can be made using wooden blocks, covering with plastic sheeting to make a floor
- a portable sand area can be made by just using a tarpaulin or plastic sheeting directly onto the ground
- it is exciting to offer at different levels such as floor or tables
- children can enjoy transporting in barrows or carts and using bucket and pulley systems
- many tools, recycled materials and containers can be used with sand
- a scenario can be set up by adults such as a treasure hunt, using magnets to find buried metal objects, playpeople or vehicles.

■ WATER

Usually easily available material – on tap! Another basic material that all babies and young children find fascinating. It supports a wide variety of learning opportunities and is deeply engaging and motivating for all children. It is important that children don't get completely soaked but must still feel able to explore the properties of water. Going swimming and bath time can be used as whole body experiences but on warm summer days in a suitable outdoor area more extensive use of water can be planned – hoses (on a sunny day you may be able to make rainbows), watering plants, using outside tap, using hand water sprayers, water painting all surfaces, footprints, puddles, splashing. In the winter take advantage of any ice or snow to extend the children's experience.

Children should learn to respect drinking water as a scarce resource in the world. Taps should be turned off and hoses not left running for long periods.

WAYS OF PRESENTING AND USING

- buckets, containers, plastic bottles, yoghurt pots all with or without holes
- graded containers
- tubes, funnels, water wheels
- things that float, corks, toy boats, plastic ducks, playpeople
- things that sink, stones, shells, keys, solid objects
- things to wash, plates, cups, dolls, socks in pairs
- adding bubbles, colour the water, sparkling things such as sequins,
- warm, icy, deep, shallow
- fish, dolphins, starfish, crabs etc.
- freeze in different containers such as balloons, rubber gloves, plastic pots of different shaped – add objects such as coins, corks, flower petals, leaves, jewellery, colouring.

■ COMPOST, STONES AND GRAVEL

Throughout the ages and in all places children have made mud pies. Garden soil can be contaminated so it is cleaner to use specially purchased materials. Garden centres are a good source. The materials can be combined in many flexible ways and again supervision and developmental age of the children is important for supervising adults to consider. Often combined with role play such as garden centres, or seaside's, these materials can also be used with small world toys such as trucks and playpeople. Seeds and cuttings can be planted in the compost.

■ CORNFLOUR

Economic when bought in large catering packs. Once mixed it can be used over 2 or 3 days if left exposed to the air. Although non toxic it will become unclean as is played with and children should be encouraged not to put in their mouths. It is a good idea for children to wear aprons and there to be washing facilities (and floor mops) nearby. If cornflour gets on clothes it will easily come out by rubbing cloth together when dry. Most children enjoy sensory exploration of this changing material. They like to observe what it can do and how it feels and to test out ideas. Using cornflour and water is a purely sensory experience with no possibility of an 'end product' as the material returns to its original flat state. If left to dry out to a powder again it can be stored and reused.

WAYS OF PRESENTING AND USING

- water in spray bottles for children to add – water may be cold or warm
- large shallow tray (concrete mixing trays can be bought relatively cheaply at builders merchants and are large enough to encourage children to make big movements and has a raised edge to contain liquid)
- plastic spatulas are effective in scooping up the liquid cornflour
- small trays
- add colouring or essences.

absorbed • excited • exploring • thoughtful
• laughing • touching • stroking
• dreaming • wallowing • chatting

mucky • runny • squelchy
• squidgy • slimy • sticky
• slippery • splodgy

Learning opportunities linked to the Early Learning Goals

These sensory activities provide opportunities for:

- **Personal, Social and Emotional Development**

  developing and extending concentration skills and high levels of involvement

  promoting a soothing and calming effect

  supporting the forming of relationships between children and adults as well between children

  playing by yourself or alongside others

- **Communication, Language and Literacy**

  exploring the words and sounds related to and evoked by the materials.

  extending vocabulary, particularly descriptive words

  talking about ideas and feelings.

  making marks

- **Mathematics**

  counting, sorting, matching, fractions

  comparison of size and shape

  capacity, volume and weight

  developing mathematical and positional language

  conservation of number, weight, volume and capacity.

- **Knowledge and Understanding of the World**

  observing change in the materials from dry to wet, solid to liquid

  exploring forces and friction

  motivating exploratory play for children at different developmental levels

- **Physical Development**

  increasing motor control and co-ordination

- **Creative Development**

  responding to touching and feeling.

  exploring texture and form

■ ROLE OF THE SUPPORTING ADULT

- to observe children's interactions with materials and each other
- to engage with the materials themselves and share the experience and the fun with the children
- to extend vocabulary and model observations of the changes in the materials
- to reassure children that it is ok to get 'mucky'
- to allow time and opportunity for all the children to feel satisfied and engaged.

■ EXTENDING

- mixing materials, such as sand and water and making connections between the materials
- explore other materials such as plaster of paris, chalk, white clay, flour and water
- involve children in cooking activities such as bread making and extending change through heat.

■ HOME LINKS

Encourage adults to participate in exploratory, fun activities with the children in a variety of ways: sand/seaside-park; gardening; cooking – mixing and preparing food; water bath time; washing clothes, toys, the car; DIY – wallpaper pasting (beware of fungicides).

Equal opportunities – access to the learning

- These activities are universally engaged in by young children and so should be gender and culture free.
- Playing with malleable materials is very therapeutic and therefore can be beneficial
- to children with sensory, neurological or emotional difficulties.
- These activities are easily adapted to meet the needs of individual children, e.g. dough on a tray, sand on the floor.

Health and safety

- Make sure that the children are not allergic to the materials – check egg boxes clean – be sure parents inform you of any allergic reactions and be vigilant.
- Children with eczema or other skin conditions may need to wear a barrier cream or only play for short periods when using materials which may dry the skin.
- Be aware that wallpaper pastes from DIY outlets usually contain fungicides – setting should obtain paste from art materials suppliers or educational catalogues
- Care should be taken with sand. Hats may be worn to avoid difficulties with hair and sand should not be thrown. (**Tip**: baseball caps stop any sand that might be thrown
- from getting into eyes as well as hair.)
- Materials should not be eaten. Extra supervision of materials such as small stones is important to ensure children do not put them in their mouths.
- Dough and other mixed materials should be renewed regularly.
- Care should be taken if dough/clay is stored in a plastic bag – it should be kept out of children's reach.
- Outdoor sandpits should be securely covered at night to prevent contamination by animals
- Children should always be supervised when playing with even shallow amounts of water.

Further reading, information and sources

Henderson, A. (1991) *Clay and Dough*, Play Activities Series. London: Pre-school Learning Alliance.

Henderson, A. (1991) *Sand and Water*, Play Activities Series. London: Pre-school Learning Alliance.

Burgess, L. (1996) *Learning through Clay and Dough*. Leamington Spa: Scholastic.

Harpley, A. and Roberts, A. (1996) *Sand*. Leamington Spa: Scholastic.

Malleable Materials NVQ links

Level 2
C 4.2, C 4.3, C 4.5, C 8.1, E 2.1, E 2.2, M 3.1, P 1.1
Level 3
C 3.4, C 5.2, C 5.3, C 7.1, C 10, C 11.1, C 11.2, C 11.4, C 11.5, C 16, E 3.4, M 7, P 2.3

FOUR

Outdoor Play

Children are active learners. They use their bodies and their senses to inform them about the world. They need space and suitable materials so that they can explore energetically. An outdoor play area is important but if not possible then opportunities should be set up for visits to parks and open spaces. Activities need to be offered which explore the natural elements of the changing seasons and the creatures that live around us. Many 'indoor' activities can also take place 'outdoors'.

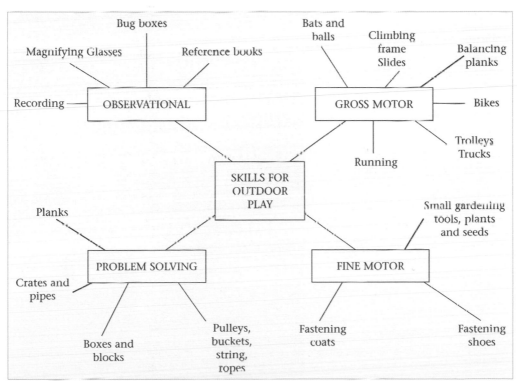

CHAPTER FOUR *Activity*

Experimenting with pipes, crates and cars

Aim: to enable children to find out about forces, speed and friction

Resources: Range of cars and small wheeled toys; different lengths of plastic guttering, pipes and plastic milk crates – can be obtained cheaply and are easily stored.

FIGURE 4.1

ADULT: *(thinking) 'How can I help the children to understand that the height of the pipe effects how fast the cars go?'*

ADULT: *(thinking) 'I must encourage S. to have a turn, she has been watching for a while*

M: *'Will the cars crash?'*

R: *'I'll catch it'*

FIGURE 4.2

ADULT: *'What will happen if we make the pipes higher?'*

ADULT: *'L's car first, M's second then R's' 'Ready, steady, go!'*

M: *'My car's got big wheels'*

L: *'We go fast in my mum's car'*

S: *'Can I catch up with my car?'*

Learning opportunities linked to the Early Learning Goals

This activity provides opportunities for:

- **Personal, Social and Emotional Development**

  co-operating and collaborating with other children of different levels of skill and ability

  satisfaction of being involved in a group

- **Communication, Language and Literacy**

  communicating ideas and explaining what is happening

  extending vocabulary

- **Mathematical Development**

  using ordinal numbers 'first . . . second . . . third'

- **Knowledge and Understanding of the World**

  observing and exploring change relating to speed, forces and friction

  experimenting and problem solving

- **Physical Development**

  moving with increased confidence and control using a range of equipment

  to handle and construct with materials

- **Creative Development**

  creating different imaginary scenarios

■ ROLE OF THE SUPPORTING ADULT

- to support the children's ideas in developing constructions
- to enable the involvement and participation of all children
- to support turn taking
- to suggest possible developments as they find solutions to their problems – using other materials (balls, water), locations (using low walls, climbing frame)
- to provide more materials for more children to actively participate.

■ EXTENDING

- add water to observe a different material and to capture and interest children
- combine with other construction materials such as hollow blocks
- link with indoor provision for example small world, construction or role play
- paint the pipes
- exploring forces and friction with other activities such as the climbing frame, ramps, bikes up and down slopes
- links with the community and extension of experience by visits to a building site or plumbers merchants.

■ HOME LINKS

- sharing the activity with parents/carers through stills and video to suggest the possibilities of using similar materials to extend and reinforce learning about forces, speed and friction at home
- encourage links with transport experiences, slides at swimming pools, holiday activities.

CHAPTER FOUR *Activity*

Observing snails

Aim: to encourage children to closely observe living creatures and find out more about them

Resources: Snails and their habitat e.g. leaves, magnifying glasses, black and white paper to help close observation, drawing paper, chalks, pens

FIGURE 4.3
KOREE: *'Look they're going in and out'* (observing snail's antenna)

BILLY: *'It goes in when I touch it'*

SAMANTHA: *'I like this round and round'* (thinking while drawing the spiral shape she has seen on the snail's shell)

FIGURE 4.4
BILLY: *'Look it's slimy'*

KOREE: *'It's moving'*

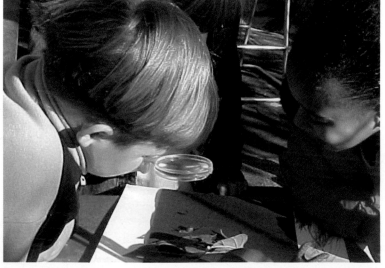

Learning opportunities linked to the Early Learning Goals

This activity provides opportunities for:

■ **Personal, Social and Emotional Development**

sharing an experience with others

developing care and respect for living creatures

involvement, curiosity, focusing and concentration

■ **Communication, Language and Literacy**

extending vocabulary

descriptions, explanations, predictions, recall

■ **Mathematical Development**

using and developing mathematical language

experiencing 3-dimensional shape, size and pattern

■ **Knowledge and Understanding of the World**

investigating and finding out about living creatures their habitat, how they move, what they eat by observation, questioning and making hypotheses

■ **Physical Development**

developing fine motor skills in handling magnifying glasses and pens

■ ROLE OF THE SUPPORTING ADULT

The children saw a snail in the nursery garden and shared this with the adults who then used their interest to develop this activity. Where such opportunities do not arise naturally adults need to introduce them.

The provision needs to be carefully planned and the children shown how to observe the creatures without harming them – to wash hands carefully if touching creatures.

■ to share the experience with the children

■ to listen and respond to children's comments and questions

■ to emphasise respect for the living snail

■ to provide further resources in the form of reference books, photographs, pictures and models.

■ EXTENDING

■ recording observations and sharing these with others through display and group times

■ keeping the snails in a perspex box for further observation of the snails, their processes and life cycle

■ exploring the shapes and pattern in different media, e.g. clay, glue and paint, sand trails, printing, dough, finger painting, bricks and blocks, patterns with pebbles

■ moving like a snail, curling up and stretching out

■ imaginative play around the theme of shells as houses/homes

■ looking at other mini beasts such as worms, caterpillars, spiders, woodlice, ants, lady birds. . .

■ HOME LINKS

■ sharing the activity through displays of children's recordings, photos and videos

■ encourage parents/carers to explore mini beasts with their children in their gardens, parks or open spaces around them

■ extend this interest in living things through involvement with pets or visits to farms and other places animals can be seen and studied.

CHAPTER FOUR *Activity*

Batting balls suspended on strings

Aim: to develop hand eye co-ordination skills and offer opportunities to use horizontal trajectory movements

Resources: Thick string and two posts or trees to tie it to
Light plastic balls of different sizes with holes
Lightweight plastic bats or children can use their hands

FIGURE 4.5
REECE: *'Mine's higher'*

JOBI: *'I hit it hard'*

DANIELLE: *'I hit it again'*

FIGURE 4.6
MICHELLE: *'My go next'*

Learning opportunities linked to the Early Learning Goals

This activity provides opportunities for:

- **Personal, Social and Emotional Development**

  turn taking and awareness of own actions and other's safety

  practising a skill independently and with perseverance

- **Communication, Language and Literacy**

  Extending vocabulary as they talk about what they are doing

- **Mathematical Development**

  developing positional language such as 'up, down, over, under, high, low'

  developing spatial awareness

- **Knowledge and Understanding of the World**

  developing practical experience of cause and effect

  developing their concepts of speed and movement through space

  problem solving when the strings get tangled up!

- **Physical Development**

  developing motor skills and muscle strength

  improving hand-eye co-ordination

ROLE OF THE SUPPORTING ADULT

- to provide the balls on strings so that they are always available and avoid the frustration of the ball disappearing every time the child hits it. It also allows for continuous practice of the skills
- to provide a range of balls such as foam to enable access by children with all levels of ability
- to site the activity in an area where there is plenty of space
- to show children how to use the bats safely and to be constantly aware of other children around them
- to encourage children's confidence to 'have a go'
- to participate in the game themselves – modelling the skills and commenting on what they are doing.

EXTENDING

- using bats and balls without string attachment – on own or in pairs
- using bats and balls against a wall
- encouraging throwing and aiming skills, e.g. into bucket or basket ball net
- developing skittle games
- using swing ball machines
- developing minor skills games such as using cricket bats and stumps, small football goal nets.

■ HOME LINKS

- share this simple idea with parents to show how active physical skills can be developed in a small space with simple equipment
- suggest using hands and soft balls/rolled up socks indoors.

Equal opportunities – access to the learning

- An adequate range of toys and equipment is needed to enable all children to choose and be fully occupied.
- Toys and equipment should be suitable to the stage of development and physical needs of the children.
- Appropriate adult involvement required to support children with different levels of ability and confidence.
- Through observation, knowledge of individual children and discussion/planning, all the adults should be aware of the need to actively ensure that boys and girls have access to all the learning opportunities.

Health and safety

- The ground surface should be in good repair and the area secure.
- A check of the trees and plants should be undertaken to ensure none have poisonous flowers or fruit.
- Daily checks for animal fouling and other hazards such as broken glass, new plants or rubbish are needed.
- All toys and equipment should be well maintained and regularly inspected.
- The layout of the outside area should consider safe movement.
- Any defective toy or piece of equipment should be removed and the adult in charge informed, notes taken and action taken.
- Co-operative work with parents/carers to ensure children are suitably clothed and shod and their skin is protected – any trailing anorak cord or jewellery, especially earrings should be removed or made safe.
- Supervising adults should be able to see all areas.
- A First Aid Box should be readily accessible in case of accidents and all adults know the routines.
- Practitioners should be aware of health need such as asthma.

Further reading, information and sources

Bilton, H. (1998) *Outdoor Play in the Early Years*. London: David Fulton

Physical Development through Play – Learn Through Play Series, Pre-school Learning Alliance

Amor, C. (1990) ed. *The Early Years: A Curriculum for Young Children – Outdoor Play*. London: Harcourt, Brace, Jovanovich.

Outdoor play NVQ links

Early Years Care & Education

Level 2

C 1.3 C 4.2 C 4.3 C 4.4 C 4.5 C 8.1 C 8.4 C 8.5 E 1.1 E 2.1 E 2.2 M 3.1 P 1.1

Level 3

C 3 C 5.2 C 5.3 C 7.1 C 7.2 C 10 C 11.1 C 11.2 C 11.4 C 11.5, E 3.1
E 3.3 E 3.4 M 7 P 2.3

Playwork

Level 2

PA 2.2 PA 3.1 PA 3.3 PA 3.4

Level 3

PB 23.1 PB 23.2 PB 23.3 PB 23.4 PC 12.2

5

Being Creative

The accent should be on individual discovery by young children using and creating with a variety of media. These materials should be easily accessed by the children therefore allowing each child to make a personal statement. The practitioner may need to help and encourage the less adventurous child to engage in the processes of experiencing and experimenting. It is important to give the children confidence by respecting their ideas and work. All children need time to explore without the stress of an expected end product from the adults. This will lead to very individual works of art that should be valued for the learning that has been involved in the process. The practitioner may wish to encourage a channelled exploration by for example giving the children a few colours or selection of materials. Sometimes it will be necessary to model techniques to enhance the children's enjoyment of the activity.

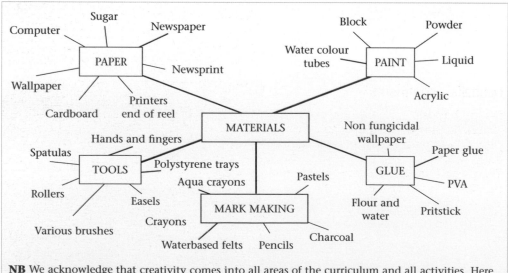

Sugar
Computer
Newspaper
PAPER
Newsprint
Wallpaper
Printers
Cardboard   end of reel

Block   Powder
Water colour
tubes   PAINT — Liquid

Acrylic

MATERIALS

Non fungicidal
wallpaper
Paper glue
Hands and fingers
Spatulas
TOOLS   Polystyrene trays
Pastels   GLUE
Rollers   PVA
Easels   Aqua crayons
Flour and
water   Pritstick
Various brushes   Crayons   MARK MAKING
Charcoal
Waterbased felts   Pencils

NB We acknowledge that creativity comes into all areas of the curriculum and all activities. Here we are focusing on being creative using media and materials.

CHAPTER FIVE *Activity*

Finger painting

Aim: to offer opportunities for a satisfying sensory experience and to develop pattern and mark making

Resources: Easily cleanable non-porous surface as appropriate to the setting – space to develop the movements is important – children can sit or stand; powder paint, paste(non fungicide), aprons, different sized pieces of paper to take prints if the children wish; hand washing facilities nearby so children can wash hands independently or adult can support.

Ryan's comments

Round and round
We're covering all the table
I'm mucky
It's cold

Adult's comments

You're going round and round with your hands
You're making big circles
It's making a circle pattern in the paint
You're hands are moving quickly
You've wiped your pattern off

Michelle's comments

It's my hands!
(Michelle pressed the paper to take a print of her painting and found her hand prints)
The paint's not moving any more
(it had dried after taking print)

Adult supportive questions

Which colour would you like first?
What's happened to the colour?
Can you use both hands?
What does it feel like?
Shall we take a print of your pattern?
Can you tell me about your
pattern/print?

Learning opportunities linked to the Early Learning Goals

This activity provides opportunities for:

- **Personal, Social and Emotional Development**

  supporting confidence to try new activities/experiences – appropriate to all stages in development

  sustained interest and absorption – a soothing, emotionally satisfying activity

  sharing their experience and feelings with others

- **Communication, Language and Literacy**

  developing descriptive language

  verbalising children's thinking and their sensory experiences

  exploring making marks and representational drawings

  developing kinaesthetic links between the brain and fingers

- **Mathematical Development**

  for using mathematical language such as big, little, circle, up, down.

- **Knowledge and Understanding of the World**

  observing processes of change as they use the materials and over time, and asking questions

  Physical Development

  developing fine motor control and co-ordination

- **Creative Development**

  exploring the use of colour and texture

  creating changing patterns which can be preserved by taking a print on paper

  making their own designs and pictures

■ ROLE OF THE SUPPORTING ADULT

- to set up the activity so that children can make choices and independently explore the process and their feelings
- to enable children to take prints if they wish to preserve a painting
- to comment on the process and the patterns to extend the children's language
- to ask what's happening to encourage further comments by the children
- to encourage the child to experiment with whole hands and with fingers to make a variety of marks and patterns

■ to support any reluctance from a child to become fully involved – reassure about the messiness and ensure children can wash hands independently or give support as necessary.

■ EXTENDING

■ building on the free movements by introducing painting with a variety of brushes and tools

■ building on the pattern making in different media – marbling, blowing painting/folding, printing, ball rolling, perspex painting, string painting, spatter painting, fly-swot painting,

■ building on the experience of colour mixing with paints, crayons

■ developing the experience of wet and dry with other materials such as adding water to dry sand, painting with water outside on a hot day, mixing dry powder paint with water, watering dry plants

■ developing sensory experiences with other materials

■ mixing cooking ingredients to combine and change.

■ HOME LINKS

■ share what the children have experienced and the learning they have achieved through the process – using display, video and photographs, to enable other adults to respect and value what the children have done

■ find other opportunities to observe and discuss similar processes at home including cooking and mixing foods

■ making opportunities to make patterns: bubbles bath, sand at the sea side, snow, mud, puddles, condensation on windows -and observing patterns in the environment in bricks, in nature – snail trails, veins on leaves.

CHAPTER FIVE *Activity*

Press printing

Aim: to give children opportunities to create a design and follow through a process to a satisfying end result

Resources: Pencil and paper for design ideas, press board from art shops/catalogues or polystyrene trays, pizza bases and packing cut to appropriate size, pointed pencil or tool, paint rollers, acrylic paint and tray to put paint in, aprons, paper, card or material to print on

FIGURES 5.4, 5.5   *A Christmas tree in a pot provided many opportunities for the children to touch and smell, to draw and paint, to talk about trees and Christmas time, to hear stories, to tell stories, to predict and recall and to decorate.*

The press printing built on this.

Charlotte was encouraged to look closely at the tree and make her own drawing.

She used her pencil to make the tree design on a segment cut from a polystyrene pizza base.

She rolled the paint over the design and printed on long strips of paper so she could see the repeat.

Later Charlotte printed on rectangular paper so she could lay out her own repeating design, she made a card for home and a copy to put in her folder.

Learning opportunities linked to the Early Learning Goals

This activity provides opportunities for:

- **Personal, Social and Emotional Development**

  involvement, engagement, concentration and satisfaction and

  commitment to finish a process

  waiting for a turn and observing others – excitement as the repeating print is revealed

- **Communication,Language and Literacy**

  listening to and following instructions

  extending vocabulary and descriptive language

  representation through mark making

- **Mathematical Development**

  exploring shape and space and creating repeating patterns, following a sequential process

  use of area as child fits in the repeats and counting how many

- **Knowledge & Understanding of the World**

  properties of materials and experience of a process of change and reversal

  use of tools – rollers rotating, pressing hard to print

  observing changes in replenishing the paint as you print

- **Physical Development**

  developing fine motor skills and control as the different materials require varying pressure

- **Creative Development**

  making own representational drawing or pattern and printing it

  creating designs with strong links to technology

■ ROLE OF THE SUPPORTING ADULT

- to provide resources and to set them up in a logical way to enable children to carry out the process independently as they become experienced
- to link with first hand experience or encourage children to represent their own ideas.

■ EXTENDING

- offering a wide selection of colours and choices of medium to print on
- printing for other purposes such as wrapping paper, materials for curtains or drapes, wallpaper for doll's house
- using other print techniques such as cutting into a soft block (not potatoes as it is wrong to teach children to 'play' with food), string patterns stuck on a block, foam shapes
- printing with patterned objects such as cotton reels, leaves, toy car tyre tracks, poppy seed heads
- using rubber stamps and ink pads
- making impressions in Plaster of Paris or clay and printing.

■ HOME LINKS

- share the process of how the children made the prints through displays, videos or photographs – some parents/carers may like to come into the setting to help develop art and craft work including sharing their own skills
- looking for examples of printing used around them at home and outside
- making links with local printers or light industry to possibly visit
- interests in hobbies such as photography and screen printing may be available locally as well in a secondary school or college.

CHAPTER FIVE *Activity*

Creating with scrap materials

Aim: to encourage children to make choices and to learn about the properties of a range of materials , to join them together to form their own creations

Resources: Materials from the scrap scheme such as ribbons, pieces of materials, boxes, papers, card, buttons, plant pots, wood and offcuts from various manufacturing processes. Recyclable materials brought in by parents and carers such as packets, tubes, containers. Plastic containers often available free from supermarkets and other retailers for displaying and storing materials so they are readily accessible. Natural materials such as leaves, conkers, twigs, shells, stones and cork. Sequins, feathers and golden/shiny papers and objects which spark off imaginative ideas and motivate the children to participate. Joining materials such as masking tape, pva glue, tags, staplers, string, wool and paper fasteners. Tools such as scissors, glue spatulas, staplers, hole punches. Access to paint and woodwork materials is useful. A storage system for multiple copies of the children's names printed from the computer so they can easily name models. (There are many times in school that children are also encouraged to recognise and to write their name/signature) A safe area where children can leave their models to dry. Pictures of other artists and sculptor's work displayed.

FIGURES 5.6, 5.7 *A large group of children working comfortably together, sharing the materials, tools and glue. The materials are arranged in small baskets on open shelves which encourage the children to thoughtfully select what they want to use.*

FIGURE 5.8 *Emily chose a very eye catching willowy golden paper, she measured how much she needed and cut it herself. She then went on to wrap up a long rectangular carton, very carefully using an appropriate amount of PVA glue to stick the edges down. She thoughtfully chose some colourful beads and feathers and arranged them attractively on the top. She selected her name label from the wall, stuck it on her model, left it on the shelf to dry and collected it at the end of the session to take home.*

Learning opportunities linked to the Early Learning Goals

This activity provides opportunities for:

- **Personal, Social and Emotional Development**

  working independently, accessing and choosing own materials, sharing tools and materials together

  encouraging persistence and concentration

  experimenting freely enables children to practice skills and extend their own learning

- **Communication, Language and Literacy**

  promoting conversational and descriptive speech.

  recognising their names.

- **Mathematical Development**

  estimating length for example how much ribbon/tape needed.

  exploring shape, space and area.

  using positional language to describe their work.

working through various schema such as enclosing and connecting

- **Knowledge and Understanding of the World**

  experiencing the properties of different materials.

  joining materials together using tools and adhesives – using tools effectively and skilfully

- **Physical Development**

  co-ordinating and strengthening muscles in the hand by using tools and small materials such as tiny beads, buttons and plastic shapes.

- **Creative Development**

  creating three dimensional structures, developing aesthetic awareness.

■ ROLE OF THE SUPPORTING ADULT

- to provide, display, replenish and renew a variety of interesting materials in an inviting way that enables children to choose easily from them and work independently
- to provide technical support where needed.

■ EXTENDING

- adults making suggestions linked to themes or interests – can you make a ladder for the fire engine, can you make an animal mask, can you make a bag for your picnic, can you make a kite to fly in the wind today
- at times limiting choices of materials to challenge their thinking
- showing examples of other artists/sculptors works
- trips to galleries and exhibitions
- provide a range of books showing the variety of creative processes.

■ HOME LINKS

- encouraging parents and carers to bring in materials to resource the area
- displaying children's creations and sharing the learning that has gone into them to ensure that the child's efforts are respected and valued
- encouraging families to visit galleries and exhibitions and explore statues or other sculptures in their area.

Equal opportunities – access to the learning

- Have available skin-tone paints and crayons for children to explore self image.
- Thick handled tools provide easier grip. Stubby brushes help with immature fine motor control and long handled rollers enable children to reach further.
- Large pieces of paper enable children with limited means of expression to participate.

- Fluorescent and tactile materials encourage visually impaired children to take part.
- Equipment should be adapted to meet the child's needs e.g. take the activity to the child on a tray. For children unable to stand unaided, easels can be lowered or tables used if a standing frame is not available.

Health and safety

- Non-toxic materials such as glue, cold water paste, paint is essential, but even so, children should not put these in their mouths. Superglue must never be used.
- Be careful not to use small polystyrone packing materials or toilet roll insides.
- Egg boxes should be perfectly clean and polystyrene trays washed thoroughly.

- Hands should be washed when the activity is completed.
- Boxes and materials brought from home are vetted to remove anything inappropriate e.g. match boxes, medicine boxes, cigarette boxes, jagged or sharp edges.
- Until the children are competent the use of round-ended scissors should be supervised at all times.

Further reading, information and sources

Henderson, A. (1998) *Paint and Print*. Play Activities Series, Pre-school Learning Alliance.

Heald, C. (1997) *Learning through Art and Craft*. Leamington Spa: Scholastic.

Leach, B. J. (1997) *Learning through Junk Materials*. Leamington Spa: Scholastic.

Henderson, A. (1991) *Glueing*. Play Activities Series, Pre-school Learning Alliance.

Duffy, B. (1998) *Supporting Creativity and Imagination in the Early Years*. Buckingham: Open University Press.

Being creative NVQ links

Level 2

C 1.4, C 4.3, C 8.1, C 8.4, E 1.2, E 2.2, M 3, P 1.1

Level 3

C 2.4, C 3.4, C 5.4, C 5.5, C 7.1, C 7.2, C 10, C 11.2, C 11.4, E 3.4, M 7, P 2.3

6

Using Technology and Materials

Children need well designed provision and support to enable them to explore the natural and the constructed world around them. They need to use things in an active way and feel secure to try things out, to make 'mistakes' and to develop the skills to solve practical problems.

Children's natural curiosity needs to be harnessed to promote progress with using learning opportunities around them. To handle things, to manipulate them to see how they work what they can do. They need adult support to encourage questioning, predicting, hypothesising and the language to explain what they can see happening.

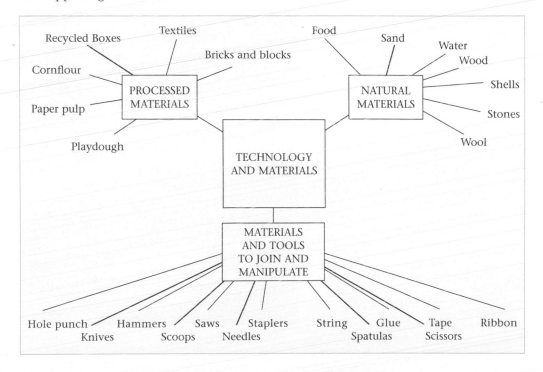

Recycled Boxes — Textiles — Food — Sand — Water — Wood

Bricks and blocks

Cornflour

PROCESSED MATERIALS — NATURAL MATERIALS — Shells

Paper pulp — Stones

Playdough — Wool

TECHNOLOGY AND MATERIALS

MATERIALS AND TOOLS TO JOIN AND MANIPULATE

Hole punch — Hammers — Saws — Staplers — String — Glue — Tape — Ribbon
Knives — Scoops — Needles — Spatulas — Scissors

CHAPTER SIX *Activity*

Using woodwork tools and materials

Aim: to give children opportunities to learn to use tools safely and appropriately with a range of materials

Resources: Child level table or bench, carpet tiles under legs and equipment to absorb sound, small sized real tools, e.g. hammers, hand drill, vice, rules, hacksaws, files, sandpaper, pincers, nails, tacks and marked places to store them. Some children may need lighter tools to start with.

A variety of materials – mostly found and scrap – cork, offcuts of soft plastic, cardboard, logs, offcuts of wood

Construction kits such as 'Tap Tap' – plastic shapes with hole, tools and task – corks mats

Brio Mec – wooden tools, strip and blocks with holes and plastic nuts and bolts.

FIGURE 6.1   *Using a hand drill*

JAMES: *'It's come off'*

SHEILAGH: *'This part fits in here*
You screw it up tightly.
Then it will work again.'

TONI: *'What are they doing?'*

FIGURE 6.2   *Using hammers*
Sheilagh and the children had just had a discussion about the difference they could feel and hear when hitting the nail in the cork or in the wood. She asked them what it was like and used words such as 'hard' 'soft' 'easy' 'noisy' and 'loud'. She asked why they thought the carpet tiles were there and they experimented together. The children then worked on independently.
James knows he must wait until Toni has finished so that he can have his turn on the table.
Toni knows she must keep her fingers away from the top ot the nail.

Learning opportunities linked to the Early Learning Goals

This activity provides opportunities for:

■ **Personal, Social and Emotional Development**

developing motivation and responsible attitudes to the safe use of tools

learning to work alongside, share resources and respect other's space

■ **Communication, Language and Literacy**

extending vocabulary

describing materials and action

■ **Mathematical Development**

developing mathematical language

gaining experience of 3-dimensional shape

learning about organising, sequencing and patterns

■ **Knowledge and Understanding of the World**

learning about the difference between natural and man-made materials

selecting appropriate tools and problem solving

■ **Physical Development**

handling tools safely with increasing control and strengthening muscles

developing hand-eye co-ordination

■ **Creative Development**

exploring and using 3-dimensional shape in their creations

opportunities to use materials imaginatively

■ ROLE OF THE SUPPORTING ADULT

■ to plan the provision carefully ensuring an appropriate range of materials are always available

■ to have oversight of this area of provision at all times

■ to show children how to use the tools and materials safely – giving set rules for safe use

■ to model effective techniques with the tools

■ to support children as they first use tools and help with any practical difficulties

■ to assess children's individual level of skill and to encourage its development

■ to provide opportunities to practise the skills – such as hammering nails into the cut surface of large logs and using vice and saw to cut off lengths of wood.

■ EXTENDING

■ gradually introduce further tools such as handsaws, screwdrivers and sandpaper as the children become more skilled

■ encourage children to progress from using soft materials such as cork and cardboard to harder ones such as wood

■ support them in their ideas to make representational objects for display and play, such as mobile phones, simple vehicles

■ support opportunities to paint and mark these, e.g. numbers on the mobile phone, decorating the vehicles.

■ HOME LINKS

■ sharing the activities with parents/carers through photos and video can suggest that they can involve their young children in 'DIY' and practical work at home

■ encourage parents/carers, extended family members such as grandparents, or others in the community with skills and time to come into the setting, maybe on a regular basis, to show how they use tools

■ parents/carers can contribute safe and suitable materials from their workplace to use at home or in the setting.

CHAPTER SIX *Activity*

Making, spreading and eating toast

Aim: to provide opportunity to observe change in materials and develop fine motor skills in a social context

Resources: Toaster, plates, round ended knives, aprons, bread – choice of types, Spread – butter or vegetable spread, honey and or other spreads e.g. jam, yeast extract, cheese spread. Hygienic surface set up in a safe area.

FIGURES 6.3, 6.4 *Bread*
Jill encouraged the children to choose which type of bread they wanted her to toast. She encouraged them to look at the bread, feel it and make predictions.

JILL: *'How does it feel?'*

CONOR: *'It's soft.*

JILL: *'Can you see it's like a square?*

Would you like white or brown?'

CONOR: *'White please.'*

Jill then turned round to the toaster behind her and showed the children how she made the toast.

FIGURES 6.5, 6 6, 0.7 *Toast*
Jill encouraged the children to
feel the toast and talk about the
changes that had happened.

JILL: *'Ooh it's hot'*

RYAN: *'It feels hot!'*
The children can spread their
own butter and honey and
enjoyed eating it.

JILL: *'Where's the butter gone?'*

TABITHA: *'It's melted.'*

Learning opportunities linked to the Early Learning Goals

This activity provides opportunities for:

- **Personal, Social and Emotional Development**

  linking with children's everyday experiences and capturing their interest and involvement

  expressing likes and dislikes – making choices

  understanding the dangers and respecting the rules

  enjoyment of participation in a social activity

  carrying out personal hygiene routines

- **Communication, Language and Literacy**

  using language to recreate their experiences

  developing comparative and descriptive language

- **Mathematical Development**

  practical experience with shape and relevant mathematical language

- **Knowledge and Understanding of the World**

  experiencing change in materials using heat

  using technology and electricity

- **Physical Development**

  developing fine motor control in spreading and cutting

  using and controlling knives

- **Creative Development**

  exploring different textures and use of senses of touch, smell and taste

■ ROLE OF THE SUPPORTING ADULT

- to set up the tables to ensure children cannot touch the hot toaster or operate the switch but so that the adult can operate the toaster while talking to the children. Setting out in a semi circle against the wall with the adult in the centre is effective but all the materials need to be at hand – the activity should never be left unattended

- to give the children choices and opportunities to develop independence whilst ensuring that the purpose of cooking and preparing to eat is successfully and appropriately achieved – we are not 'playing' with food and children stay seated to eat

- to assesses the level of physical skill and response of the children and offer appropriate support

- to encourage the children to observe and comment, to listen to and watch each other.

■ EXTENDING

- cutting the bread into different shapes and fractions such triangles and quarters – using the appropriate language

- visits to bakers – looking at and tasting breads from around the world

- setting up an interest table with the stages and processes of flour and bread making – corn to flour to dough

- linking with stories such as 'The Little Red Hen'

■ making bread using yeast and showing the process

■ making playdough with flour and water (comparing with yeast process) plaiting and making small buns and loaves, bake, paint and use in domestic role play

■ make sandwiches with different fillings and toasted sandwiches

■ extending cutting skills in vegetable soup making

■ eating soup and bread you have made together at lunchtime or invite visitors in to share

■ using the concept of melting from heat with water and ice

■ participating in other cooking activities using other technology such as microwaves, pasta machines, blenders and small portable cookers.

■ HOME LINKS

■ sharing with parents the children's levels of skill and competence so that they will find time at home to involve them in cooking or preparing picnics, lunchboxes etc.

■ encouraging children to make choices for healthy eating.

CHAPTER SIX *Activity*

Joining materials together

Aim: to enable children to experiment with a range materials in order to understand their properties and to gain skills in joining them

Resources: A range of recycled materials such as cardboard, plastic boxes, offcuts, papers, straws(make use of your local scrap scheme)

A range of hole making tools such as punches and scissors and fixing materials such as staples, tags, pva liquid glue, glue sticks, masking tape, clear sticking tape, plastic tapes

6.9

6.8

6.11

6.10

FIGURES 6.8, 6.11 *Working in the graphics area on their own products/ideas*

FIGURES 6.9, 6.10 *Working in the technology area making ladders linked to the theme of fire safety*

Learning opportunities linked to the Early Learning Goals

These activities provide opportunities for:

- **Personal, Social and Emotional Development**

  gaining confidence to use tools safely and materials, to make choices and concentrate

  to initiate and use ideas, to try new things

- **Communication, Language and Literacy**

  using language to explain the processes and what they are doing – on, under, up, round,

  developing vocabulary with the names of tools and materials and describing what is happening

  writing and using name labels to personalise their products

- **Mathematical Development**

  using 3-D shapes

  understanding concepts such as estimation and prediction

  creating and recognising patterns

- **Knowledge and Understanding of the World**

  problem solving through trial and error

  making prediction and judgements

  noticing and using similarities and differences

  choosing the appropriate tools to put together the materials in their constructions

- **Physical Development**

  developing motor skills increasing control and confidence in handling tools and achieving their objectives

- **Creative Development**

  making things in 2 and 3 dimensions

  representing through modelling and using their imagination

■ ROLE OF THE SUPPORTING ADULT

- to provide a large range of tools and plentiful supply of materials to allow all the children opportunities to participate and try out their ideas
- to support the child in their constructions by helping develop practical skills without imposing adults own ideas or constraints, listening carefully and intervening when appropriate
- to join in and work alongside the children on their own projects – describing what they are doing and commenting positively on the children's work and ideas.

■ EXTENDING

- keeping and displaying some of each child's work to enable reflection, discussion and developing ideas
- making books
- mending and fixing things around the setting as appropriate
- working together in making presents and items for others on special occasions and festivals – such as Chinese dragons for the dragon dance, divas, fans, cards,
- encouraging children to select and refill supply of materials to discuss what they need and how it could be contained.

■ HOME LINKS

- sharing and valuing what the children make
- collecting materials to use at home and to bring in to contribute to resources in the setting
- encouraging adults to share their hobbies and skills with the children and involving them at their level.

Equal opportunities – access to the learning

- adequate range of materials and equipment to enable all children to choose and be fully occupied
- activities to be suitable to stage of development
- adequate adult involvement to support children with different levels of ability and confidence
- adaptation of activity to accommodate all

- children including those with physical disabilities
- adults through observation and planning should ensure that boys and girls have equal access
- cooking ingredients should take into account the cultural and dietary requirements of the children
- utensils should reflect the cultural diversity

Health and safety

- activities need to be carefully planned in order that children may be supervised at all times
- children should be shown the correct way to handle tools and equipment
- tools should be age appropriate
- electrical equipment should be placed out of children's' reach
- cooking surfaces should be clean and

- adults and children's hands should be washed
- allergies should be taken into account when planning a cooking activity
- all equipment must be regularly checked for faults and defective equipment removed, notes made and appropriate action taken
- materials should be vetted for safety, e.g. nails in wood

Further reading, information and sources

Henderson, A. (1991) *Glueing*. Play Activities Series, Pre-school Learning Alliance.

Henderson, A. (1992) *Technology Through Play*. Learning Through Play Series, Pre-school Learning Alliance.

Henderson, A. (1991) *Maths Through Play*. Learning Through Play Series, Pre-school Learning Alliance.

Leach, B. (1997) *Learning through Junk Materials*. Leamington Spa: Scholastic.

Gura P. (1996) *Resources for Early Learning – Children, Adults and Stuff*. London: Hodder & Stoughton.

Pre-school Learning Alliance (1997) What Do we Mean by Maths?

using technology and materials NVQ links

Level 2

C 1.1, C 1.2, C 4.3, C 4.5, C 8.1, C 8.3, C 8.4, E 1.1, E 2.1, E 2.2, M 3.1, P 1.1

Level 3

C 2.1, C 2.2 C 3.4, C 5.3, C 7.1, C 7.2, C 10, C 11.2, C 11.4, C 11.5, C 16, E 3.1, E 3.3, E 3.4, M 7, P 2.3

7

Construction and Imagination

From very early in their lives babies and children actively find pleasure in building with things around them. They explore the properties of objects and how they relate to each other. They are in control of the things they construct and this helps them to become involved and confident. They derive pleasure from their achievements and their constructions help adults to value the children's thinking and abilities.

Children can negotiate with other children and learn from each other as they develop their play. Simple resources can provide endless imaginative experiences for the children. Different size cardboard boxes stimulate their imagination and allow them to freely express their ideas and construct their own imaginary world. In early years settings the provision of recyclable materials such as boxes, of all sizes, commercial waste (safe and non-toxic recycled materials can be obtained through Scrap Schemes and Projects), lengths of fabric, empty crates and other 'stuff' (Pat Gura, 1996) should be rich and varied. It is important that quality blocks and construction toys are a priority in spending plans. It is a good idea to invest in these rather than a little of many different sorts of equipment. You can never have enough.

Blankets   Saris   Curtaining
Cloth/woven materials

Natural materials

Big stones   Shells

Leaves   Cones   Small logs

RECYCLED
MATERIALS

Cardboard & plastic

Boxes Tubes Crates Pipes/guttering
(get friendly with your local dairy)

COMMERCIAL CONSTRUCTION
MATERIAL

Bau Play Brio Mec sets Lego/Duplo Polydron Community Playthings blocks & hollow blocks
Mobilo   Lasy   PolyM   Tree Blocks   Stickle Bricks   Popoids

CHAPTER SEVEN *Activity*

Building with Blocks

Aim: To learn the properties of the material and to use them in imaginative ways

Resources: As large a selection of good quality wooden bricks and blocks as possible – these need to be well made. They need to fit together geometrically (an ideal range is made by Community Playthings).

A storage system can be developed to enable children to access and replace blocks easily. For example, fitting them into a storage box or matching them onto outline shapes on a shelf.

A range of play people and vehicles can be available for the children.

FIGURE 7.1 *Shuoh-Fuu is balancing carefully. He was keen to build the tower higher than himself. He was very proud of what he had made and many people came to admire his tower. It was fun when it collapsed and he enjoyed rebuilding it. He was keen to share his experience with others and until this day Shuoh-Fuu had not spoken much at nursery.*

FIGURE 7.2 *Ryan and William became very involved in building furniture. It involved them in lots of discussion and helped to develop their imaginative play.*

FIGURE 7.3   *Ryan, Georgia, Aman and Jamie made a fire station, roads and buildings for the fire engines. They revisited this every day for around two weeks, making connections with a current theme.*

Learning opportunities linked to the Early Learning Goals

This activity provides opportunities for:

- **Personal, Social and Emotional Development**

  deeply satisfying involvement for all children

  individuals or small groups working together

  developing respect for other's constructions – that it is wrong to alter or destroy another person's work

- **Communication Language and Literacy**

  communication of ideas and interaction with others both verbally and visually

  expression in a non verbal way where children have English as an additional language or a language delay/disorder

- **Mathematical Development**

  problem solving and exploration using 3-dimensional shape

  developing the use of mathematical language e.g. 'high as' and positional language such as 'on top of'

  developing spatial awareness

  experience using symmetry, shape, balance, sorting, matching and classifying

  creating a visual awareness of mathematical relationships, eg two semi-circles make a circle

- **Knowledge and Understanding of the World**

  working through problem solving issues which interest them

  taking 'risks' as there need not be an expected outcome – this allows for revisiting and redesigning of ideas and processes

- **Physical Development**

  increasing co-ordination and control of their bodies as the children develop their constructions

- **Creative Development**

  increasing imagination in their designs and expressing ideas and feelings

  exploring form and shape

■ ROLE OF THE SUPPORTING ADULT

- to ensure storage, provision and accessibility of blocks.and place in a suitable environment where exploration can go on for long periods without interruption
- to allow children to return to the activity to extend their play
- to value children's ideas and discuss their ideas with them
- to give ideas and techniques to enable children to continue and develop their skills
- to model mathematical and positional language as the children build
- to record the children's ideas and processes by drawing plans, scribing anecdotes and by taking photographs.

■ EXTENDING

- responding to children's ideas and interests by helping them to use blocks in different areas of the setting, indoors and out, integrating with other activities
- making drawings of their models to make a record of their building – adults can annotate so the children's ideas are communicated
- to enable some children to develop skills which enable them to plan and record what they are going to build.

■ HOME LINKS

- sharing the children's achievements and skills with parents
- encourage building with a range of materials at home
- encourage observation and discussion about the buildings in the locality.

CHAPTER SEVEN *Activity*

Imaginative play with boxes and blankets

Aim: to enable children to use construction materials in imaginative ways

Resources: Different sized boxes and blankets and/or pieces of material/ mats or pieces of carpet

Other resources can be added as the children come up with ideas e.g.: teaset, dressing up clothes and hats

FIGURES 7.5, 7.6, 7.7, 7.8 *Hiding in boxes*
Children very often like to find spaces to hide away in, to be on their own, to be away from adults. To be in their own little world and be in control, to daydream, to be still to think up stories. Feeling cosy, safe and cocooned inside a box with a blanket.
Time for a quiet chat
The boxes are easily moved by the children to create different arrangements and dens.

Learning opportunities linked to the Early Learning Goals

This activity provides opportunities for:

- **Personal, Social and Emotional Development**

  playing alone or as part of a group – developing a sense of fun and relaxation

  formation of friendships and to play amicably

  building the confidence to try new experiences and try out their own ideas

  children who are interested in hiding, enclosing and enveloping schemas

- **Communication, Language and Literacy**

  exciting new experiences which will generate communication especially about their thoughts and feelings

  describing their environment, using prepositions – up, down, under, through

  fuelling their imagination and developing their own narratives

- **Mathematical Development**

  using mathematical language such as bigger, smaller

  developing concepts of number, size, space, volume, capacity, weight and area

- **Knowledge And Understanding of the World**

  learning about the properties of the resources

- **Physical Development**

  developing body awareness and control

  promoting flexibility

- **Creativity**

  symbolic play, allowing their imaginations to develop and engage in fantasy play

  pretend play without adult directed outcomes using an open ended resource

ROLE OF THE SUPPORTING ADULT

- to collect a range of interesting boxes, to provide a safe space for play and to stand back and watch allowing time for play to develop
- to observe social interaction, communication and negotiation skills
- to intervene to help resolve conflict where necessary.

EXTENDING

- using a range of boxes to experiment with ideas of conservation for example big light boxes, small heavy boxes
- looking at packaging, what the box used to contain and investigating the print.
- creating a display of different boxes, treasure boxes, story boxes, family box of memories
- making, decorating and filling their own boxes
- modelling with recycled materials
- looking at people's homes around the world and through history
- using boxes for other purposes such as an obstacle course including joining together to make a tunnel
- developing the mathematical language and problem solving with the boxes
- making links with songs stories poems for example 'My Cat Likes to Hide in Boxes'.

HOME LINKS

- sharing with parents/carers the value and opportunities of this resource
- encouraging them to use at home and to bring in to the setting.

CHAPTER SEVEN *Activity*

Building with Mobilo

Aim: to use the material to design and make their own models

Resources: appropriate amounts of Mobilo to allow the children choice and for some models to be kept; containers to present categories of the pieces, e.g. wheels, connectors, blocks; laminated pictures of constructed models

FIGURE 7.9   *Koree is interested in connecting the cubes*

FIGURE 7.10   *Tremaine has made a model of a helicopter with a pilot and is interested in making the parts move*

Learning opportunities linked to the Early Learning Goals

TThis activity provides opportunites for:

- **Personal, Social and Emotional Development**

  producing satisfying results

  involvement and concentration

  sharing and co-operating

- **Communication, Language and Literacy**

  making links with storytelling using the representational models,

- **Mathematical Development**

  using and naming 3 dimensional shapes

  counting,matching and sorting

  noticing similarities and differences

  using prepostional language

  following pictorial instructions

- **Knowledge and Understanding of the World**

  planning and designing models

  investigating ways of connecting the material and making models which move

  understanding the properties and functions of the different parts of the construction toy

- **Physical Development**

  developing fine motor control and hand-eye co-ordination

- **Creative Development**

  using their imagination to construct and use representational models and through these communicate ideas and feelings

ROLE OF THE SUPPORTING ADULT

- to present all the parts of the toy in an accessible way
- to support children's confidence in exploring and using, enabling continuity and deep involvement
- to ensure children have opportunities to concentrate for long periods and to revisit the material frequently
- to value children's ideas
- to display children's models and writing about their ideas and how they built them.

EXTENDING

- encouraging children to draw their model as a record
- photographing children's models and having these available as a visual resource for other children
- linking with current themes and interests, e.g. fire engines, moving models
- sharing photographs and paintings to show how design has changed over time
- encouraging children who are developmentally ready to plan before they build by discussion or drawing.

HOME LINKS

- sharing what the children have made and encouraging adults to become involved in model making at home
- involving children in adult skills in model making and DIY (use of tools and materials)
- encourage visits to exhibitions of models or collections of vehicles past and present

Equal opportunities – access to the learning

- Girls should be encouraged to play in this area as it is sometimes seen as stereotypically led towards boys.
- Small scale activities can be easily adapted and taken to a child for play on a tray where use of textured cloth would prevent slipping.

- Foam wedges or air mattresses can be used to support a child on the floor.
- Construction is a universally enjoyed activity by young children and there should be no cultural issues in these activities.

Health and safety

- Ensure rules are adhered to, eg no throwing, no putting small pieces in mouths.
- There should be enough hazard-free space to enable large-scale construction.
- A rug or carpet on the floor will provide comfort.
- Wooden blocks should be checked for splinters.
- Plastic construction materials should be washed regularly.
- Boxes should be checked for staples.

Further reading, information and sources

Heald, C. (1997) *Learning through Construction Play*. Leamington Spa: Scholastic.

Gura. P. (1990). *Exploring Learning: Young Children and Block Play*. London: Paul Chapman Publishing.

Video Bruce .T. (1992). 'Building a Future: Block Play and Young Children'. The Froebel Block Play Research Group (VIDEO).

'Criteria for Play Equipment'. Community Playthings, Robertsbridge, East Sussex, England TN32 5DR

Construction NVQ Links

Level 2

C 1.4, C 4.2, C 4.3, C 4.5, C 8.1, C 8.4, C 9.3, E 1.1, E 2.1, E 2.2, M 3.1, P 1.1

Level 3

C 3.3, C 3.4, C 5.2, C 5.3, C 7.2, C 10, C 11.2, C 11.4, E 3.1, E 3.3, M 7, P 2.3

EIGHT

Small World Play

Miniature worlds fascinate people of any age. Many adults still enjoy model trains, model villages or build models of aeroplanes and space ships. Collections of miniature houses, thimbles, vintage cars involve much absorption, time and energy. It has lot to do with self-esteem and how people view themselves in relation to the world.

Models of farms, trains, airports and dolls houses can help young children find out how things work, or how the adult world functions.

Small world play allows young children to be in control and to act out any worries or feelings. It enables them to express ideas and develop dramatic situations.

Small figures, puppets, superheroes, dolls and tiny objects can provide the means for children to escape into a fantasy world. To imagine what it might feel and be like to be part of that world and work through feelings and ideas

At times small figures or models can assume great importance to young children. They may need to keep them with them in different settings, transporting them between places and on journeys.

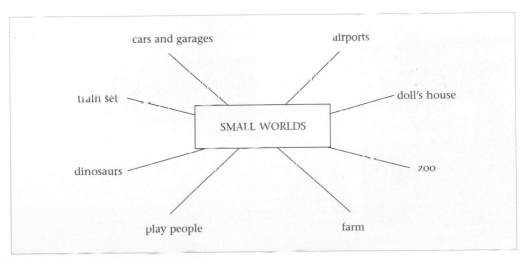

CHAPTER EIGHT *Activity*

Playing with playpeople, trucks and salt

Aims: to provide opportunities for imaginary and exploratory play

Resources: Shallow tray (ones for cement mixing can be bought cheaply), cooking salt (as a general principle we do not use items that children know are food – such as out of date pasta/rice, old apples/potatoes – in play activities but we do use widely available ingredients such as this salt, flour in playdough and cornflour which are reused many times. We use water as a essential element for children to explore and experiment with but use every opportunity to talk about waste and conserving resources) Play people – the items shown are from a workman set with miniature spades, brushes and other tools. Small vehicles such as tipper trucks, diggers, road rollers etc.

FIGURES 8.1, 8.2   *Sam and his twin brother Reece are deeply absorbed in scooping up the salt with miniature spades and diggers. They concentrated for a long period and developed their play.*

FIGURE 8.3   *Samantha was engaged in sweeping the salt with a miniature broom and became interested in the pattern she was making.*

Learning opportunities linked to the Early Learning Goals

This activity provides opportunities for:

- **Personal, Social and Emotional Development**

  emotionally satisfying play with no external demands, the child is in control

  opportunities to be comfortable playing alongside or sharing with other children

  extending concentration and levels of involvement (Leuven Scales)

- **Communication, Language and Literacy**

  using language to imagine and recreate roles and experiences

  interacting with other children and sequencing scenarios

  mark making in the salt

- **Mathematical Development**

  matching, sorting and classifying objects

  developing spatial concepts and using prepositions

  pattern making

- **Knowledge and Understanding of the World**

  representing the 'real' world on a small scale and for children to be in control of it

  exploration of the properties of materials and cause and effect through pulling and pushing

- **Physical Development**

  developing fine motor control and manipulative skills

- **Creative Development**

  responding to materials and expressing thoughts, feelings and experiences

  building imaginative scenarios – clearing away the snow and making tracks with vehicles

■ ROLE OF THE ADULT

- to provide a range of resources and structures to support the play scenarios – these can be commercial sets of toys or hand made from found materials, peg dolls, knitted items
- to make links with children's experiences in the local community
- to observe children as they play uninterrupted in order to assess their level of involvement and skills
- to join in alongside the children to add vocabulary and model possible extensions based on observation
- to help children deal with conflict.

■ EXTENDING

- adding different resources in response to the children's ideas and needs, e.g. small bricks and blocks to build with, road signs, small houses/garages, other small figures
- helping children to add resources they make such as small boxes, and other recyclable materials
- exploring the properties of salt – adding water and dissolving

- developing mark making in the salt and recording as part of the play – signs and notices
- offering other playpeople and materials such as hospital play, fire fighters, space stations, pirates, vehicles
- tune into current Super Hero and television interests to develop play scenarios and narratives with figures.

■ HOME LINKS

- asking parents/carers to supply resources such as sawdust/wood shavings
- sharing parents/carers occupations and knowledge to develop play scenarios and involving them in this
- sharing with parents/carers the potential of small world play and how they could develop at home and make links with the setting.

CHAPTER EIGHT *Activity*

Playing with small world animals

Aims: to provide opportunities for imaginative play and developing knowledge of animals and habitats

Resources: A large selection of wild (not tame or pets) animals and props to recreate the habitat, large sheets or rolls of paper, a variety of pens, crayons, pencils, etc., table or floor area. Story books and reference books about wild animals , tape recorder and recording of song 'walking through the jungle'.

FIGURES 8.4, 8.5   *Saba Ikhlas has drawn water for the elephant to drink*

FIGURE 8.6 *Children sharing the experience of drawing their own jungle scene together*

Learning opportunities linked to the Early Learning Goals

This activity provides opportunities for Development:

- **Personal, Social and Emotional**

    playing alone or co-operating with other children

    concentration and deep involvement

    expressing their feeling and emotions through the actions of the animals

    making choices in selecting materials and being confident enough to experiment and take risks

- **Communication, Language and Literacy**

    using language to classify animals and recreate their sounds

    talking about children's experiences with animals

    recording and developing their own ideas and stories through mark making and pictures

- **Mathematical Development**

    matching, sorting, counting and classifying animals

    simple addition and subtraction

- **Knowledge and Understanding of the World**

    finding out about the animal world and recreating it, understanding and respecting the needs of other species

    looking at similarities and differences

- **Physical Development**

    developing fine manipulative control and manipulative skills

- **Creative development**

    expressing and recreating their responses to the models and music on paper or in story form, and developing their own creations

■ ROLE OF THE ADULT

- to provide a range of wild animals, props and materials for recording their play
- to extend the children's vocabulary by naming, describing and classifying animals
- to encourage children to talk about visits to the zoo, safari parks, farms, pets etc. and the differences between tame and wild animals.

■ EXTENDING

Possible extensions of this activity are:

- using as part of an animal theme and extending to other animals, fish, birds etc.
- reading stories about animals and recreating the stories using props
- singing animal songs and saying rhymes
- visiting zoos, farms or animal experts bringing live animals into the setting
- developing role play areas such as a vet's surgery or an animal sanctuary
- using lotto games involving animal sounds and recognition
- offering sessions developing ideas of animal movements
- exploring animal theme through masks, drama, puppets and model making.

■ HOME LINKS

- encourage families to visit zoos, safari parks and farms and viewing together wild life programmes/videos
- sharing the care and needs of pets and garden animals.

CHAPTER EIGHT *Activity*

Playing with a train set

Aim: to provide opportunities for imaginative play involving construction of tracks and movement of trains

Resources: Clean, even area of floor with optional pre-printed mat; wooden train set comprising straight and curved track, bridges, tunnels, engines, carriages and wagons, wooden bricks for buildings

---

FIGURE 8.7   *Ben pushes the train through the tunnel onto the track he has built as an extension to the set layout*

FIGURE 8.8 *Ben is pulling the train through the other side of the tunnel*

FIGURE 8.9 *Hudaifah and Ben are moving the train up to the turntable*

FIGURE 8.10 *Luke and Amiee discuss where the train is going*

Learning opportunities linked to the Early Learning Goals

This activity provides opportunities for:

■ **Personal, Social and Emotional Development**

playing alone, alongside, fosters co-operation through negotiation of shared resources

concentrating and involvement – the movement can be soothing and absorbing

■ **Communication, Language and Literacy**

developing positional language such as on, under, over and through

creating stories and making links with known train stories

■ **Mathematical Development**

creating or recreating patterns when constructing the layout beyond or when there is no set layout

using mathematical language such as curved, straight slow and fast

sorting, matching and counting

■ **Knowledge and Understanding of the World**

exploring motion, balance and forces including the attracting and repelling action of magnets on ends of train pieces.

problem solving in constructing track using straight, curved and joining pieces

■ **Physical Development**

developing fine manipulative skills and flexible movements

■ **Creative Development**

using imagination to make up stories in relation to the play

■ ROLE OF THE ADULT

■ to provide appropriate amounts of resources and space
■ to encourage discussion about children's own experiences
■ to play alongside where appropriate and to comment on what you and the children are doing
■ to intervene where necessary or requested.

■ EXTENDING

■ provide variety of props such as play people, cars
■ extend interest with other train sets and vehicles
■ provide first hand experience of trains and travelling on them
■ set up linked role play scenarios such as a ticket office, railway station, with boxes, chairs or blocks to represent a passenger train
■ make tickets, signs and notices
■ make plans, maps and models
■ read stories and sing songs – adapt where necessary e.g. 'the wheels on the train'
■ include in wheeled theme and look at other modes of transport
■ trace the history of the train and include trams
■ visit from schools liaison officer to talk about safety on the railways.

■ HOME LINKS

■ encourage families to visit local railway stations and preserved railways

■ encourage adults to share interest and knowledge of trains and real and model railways.

Equal opportunities – access to the learning

■ play figures should represent a wide variety of cultures, disabilities, family styles and non-gender stereotyping, e.g. female fire fighters, male nurses

■ use of larger play figures allows easier grip for children with fine motor difficulties

■ all children should have the opportunity to play with a wide range of small world toys, e.g. girls with cars and trains and boys with dolls houses

Health and safety

■ Care should be taken that children do not put small pieces in their mouths.

■ Equipment should be checked regularly for cleanliness and broken pieces removed.

■ Activities which include salt and other such

material must be carefully supervised so children do not get it in their eyes or on broken skin, be aware of any allergies.

■ Spilt salt or sand should be swept from the floor to minimise slipping.

Further reading, information and sources

Julie Lacome (1993). *Walking Through the Jungle*. London: Walker Books
Game Songs with Prof Dogg's Troupe 1985. London: A.C. Black Ltd. (song book).
Leach, B. (1997). *Learning through Small World Play*. Leamington Spa: Scholastic.
Henderson, A. (1991). *Make Believe Play*. Play Activities Series. Pre-school Learning Alliance.

Small world NVQ links

Level 2
C 1.4, C 4.2, C 4.3, C 4.4, C 4.5, C 9.3, E 2.2, P 1.1
Level 3
C 2.4, C 3.4, C 5.2, C 5.3, C 5.4, C 5.5, C 7.1, C 10.1, C 10.3, C 10.4, C 11.1, C 11.2, C 11.4, C 11.5, C 15.1, M 7, P 2.3

9

Sharing Stories, Playing Imaginatively and Making Marks

Everybody loves stories and can become absorbed in them. We tell 'stories' every day as we describe incidents and scenarios. Telling and listening to stories is an essential element in language development. It is a delightful and satisfying experience to give to children. It needs to involve children one to one with an adult, in small groups and between themselves. They must feel comfortable and secure, be able to see illustrations and text or other objects. They need to be engaged and settled quietly in a place and at a time when they can listen and pay attention. Quiet areas, soft music, looking at books themselves and seeing adults reading for their own pleasure.

Not all children are ready to sit in a large story group for long periods so this experience needs to be built up sensitively and led by the children's needs not matters of management, control or organisation. A variety of books in a variety of formats, authors, illustrators need to be consistently available to children indoors and outdoors. Some stories should reflect the culture the children live in and give positive images of gender and culture. Some stories and print should be written in various scripts (dual text books are now widely available) and told in a variety of languages to respect and value the enrichment the children and families bring. Parents, carers and others in the community speaking additional languages may be invited to come into the setting to share and tell stories

Stories help children to recognise and articulate ideas or feelings that they have been experiencing. Settings need to offer a variety of means of accessing stories for children with different levels of development and language. Story props (small toys related to the characters/objects in the story) or pictures with magnetic strips on, enable children to replay, understand and recreate the story and ideas involved whatever their level of language development.

There are many kinds of stories linking reality and fantasy. Some stories even give suggestions to children about how to deal with unhappy or uncomfortable situations. Stories for young children usually end happily by giving characters new achievements or giving the children a satisfactory sense of completion.

Children learn that print and words carry meaning. They link to the print around them and the marks they and others make. A language rich environment and adults who value and use words and print need to encompass children from within weeks of birth.

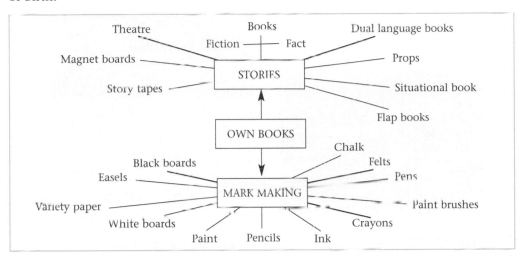

CHAPTER NINE *Activity*

Using story props with a big book of the story of The Three Bears And Goldilocks

Aim: to engage a small group of children in sharing and enjoying a traditional story

Resources: Comfortable space on the floor or with low level chairs.
   Big book of Goldilocks and The Three Bears and small books of the same story. Props.
   Time for children to come and join in and develop their storying skills during the session.

FIGURE 9.1 *Karen, a parent helper, invites the children to participate. She reads the story and draws attention to the pictures and text. She responds to the children's contributions and encourages them to interact with the props.*

FIGURE 9.2 *Lauren has a little book of Goldilocks and is following the sequence. She is running her finger under the print. Natalie helps Goldilocks to eat the porridge.*

FIGURE 9.3 *The children can play with the props on their own and retell the story.*

Learning opportunities linked to the Early Learning Goals

This activity provides opportunities for:

- **Personal, Social and Emotional Development**

  promoting enjoyment and emotional involvement, thereby building up concentration.

  building children's' confidence to join in and respond

  developing awareness of their own and other's feelings

  beginning to develop an awareness of what is right and wrong

  being physically still, quiet and absorbed

- **Communication, Language and Literacy**

  developing a disposition to listen and respond

  exploring and playing with language and extending vocabulary

  developing an understanding of sequential patterns, the rhythm and repetition within the story using their memory to begin to retell the story

  firing their imagination to make up their own stories

  developing an awareness of print, that it carries meaning and begin to respond to familiar words and letters and a knowledge of how books work

- **Mathematical Development**

  sequencing and pattern making

  concepts of size and number – small, medium, big – the threeness of three plus one

  one to one correspondence – matching the size of bear to the bowl, chair and bed

- **Knowledge And Understanding of the World**

  links with traditional tales

  awareness of hot and cold/ hard and soft

- **Physical Development**

  turning pages and manipulating props helps co-ordination

- **Creative Development**

  responding to a story using their senses and using expressive voices

  promoting imagination and creating their own dramatic stories

■ ROLE OF THE SUPPORTING ADULT

- ■ to plan and initiate the activity providing the books and props
- ■ to invite the children to participate, to listen and respond, to interact with the props and retell the story in a variety of ways
- ■ to give time for revisiting the story for as long as the children are interested, leaving the props and the books (including different versions) for the children to use themselves, to retell and create their own stories.

■ EXTENDING

- ■ set up a role play area for the story
- ■ make links to other areas of learning –
  – Can you make a bowl/chair/bed – from clay/plasticine/blocks/found materials
  – Mark making and creating books for example, write a shopping list for mummy bear, make a list of presents for baby bear's birthday
  – Find out about real bears
  – Use other books about bears and sing related songs e.g. When Goldilocks went to the house of the bears/ The three bears rap/ A bear went over the mountain/ Isn't it funny how a bear likes honey/ Teddy Bear's Picnic
  – Make porridge/honey sandwiches/toast
  – Links to numbers and size e.g. The Three Billy Goats/The Three pigs.

■ HOME AND COMMUNITY LINKS

- ■ share children's interests through photos, books and props to borrow
- ■ invite parents to share traditional stories and stories from cultural traditions.

■ EXTENDING THE WORK WITH THE THREE BEARS

Following several group story sessions using various versions of the story of Goldilocks and The Three Bears, the props are left for the children to use independently during the session.

FIGURE 9.4 *Here Alcin, Aman and Nathanial are absorbed in sharing the story together. They are co-operating well and taking turns with the props. Retelling the story sequence and matching sizes of bowls, chairs, beds and bears the children are developing a wide range of mathematical and linguistic skills.*

FIGURES 9.5, 9.6, 9.7   *Staff led several session in the block play area encouraging children to build beds for bears and some children revisited this activity many times. Amy was particularly adventurous in building a bunk bed for baby bear. Her constructional skills are well developed as she balances the structure carefully. She thoughtfully provides baby bear with a pillow and his pot of honey in case he gets hungry in the middle of the night.*

FIGURE 9.8   *A taped version of the story was left on a table under the veranda in the garden for children to listen to as they chose. A set of small wooden bricks was provided so they could continue making beds for the bears as they listened to the story. The book was there and paper and pencils should they wish to draw or write.*

FIGURES 9.9, 9.10, 9.11 *Clark and Danielle decided to make a special picnic for baby bear as it was his birthday. They gathered all the plates, cups, dishes and food – Including a plastic birthday cake with candles and transported them to another carpet area. They also wrapped presents for him and this play was developed uninterrupted over a whole session. Adults joined the picnic then supported the tidying away of the picnic.*

CHAPTER NINE *Activity*

Sari games: sharing an interactive story

Aim: to engage children actively in a story sequence

Resources: Book *Sari Games* by Naina Gandhi publisher Andre Deutsch; comfortable space, a sari (parents/carers give us their old saris for children to use and play with), Indian music helps the dance and imaginative sections of the story, picnic things, books to read under the tent.

FIGURE 9.12 *Beginning the story*

FIGURE 9.13 *It was a rainy day and the children could not play ball in the garden, so a boy's mother showed the children an indoor ball game using the Sari. All the children enjoyed taking part.*

FIGURES 9.14, 9.15 *The children dress up as Super Heroes in the sari and the mother makes the boy into a prince with a turban.*

FIGURE 9.16 *The sari becomes a sea then a river and all the children sit down and have a picnic.*

FIGURE 9.17 *Then they curl up under the sari blanket to go to sleep*

FIGURE 9.18 *The children are tired so make a tent of the sari, go inside and look at books*

Learning opportunities linked to the Early Learning Goals

This activity provides opportunities for:

- **Personal, Social and Emotional Development**

  enjoying being part of a group and respecting each others cultures

  developing co-operation and turn taking, concentration and involvement

  promoting self esteem and the confidence to take an active part

- **Communication, Language and Literacy**

  listening and responding – connecting the actions in the storybook with their playing

- **Mathematical Development**

  following the sequence of the story

  using mathematical language, especially involving length and spatial awareness

- **Knowledge and Understanding of the World**

  awareness of each other's cultures

  varied use of materials

- **Physical Development**

  increased motor control and co-ordination

- **Creative Development**

  nurturing and giving expression to children's imagination

  taking on different roles and acting out the story

■ ROLE OF THE SUPPORTING ADULT

- to plan how to use the story and gather the props with the children
- involving and enthusing all the children in the group
- responding positively to children's suggestions
- supporting the children's efforts to play out the situations in the book with the sari.

■ EXTENDING

- encouraging children to develop other ways of using the sari and create their own scenarios
- take photographs of the children playing the out the story sequence and making into a book for later recall
- have saris available for dressing up
- link resources that reflect the Asian way of life, for example cooking utensils, foods
- link to festivals such as Divali
- look at clothes communities wear around the world.

■ HOME LINKS

- encouraging parents to share their cultural traditions, for example showing children how saris are worn, bringing in and cooking food, celebrating festivals.
- sharing traditional tales from diverse cultures, e.g. Babushka, Rama and Sita, Chinese Dragon, Anansi
- looking at print in a variety of languages
- encouraging parents/carers to take children on visits to restaurants, places of worship and shops/markets.

CHAPTER NINE *Activity*

Using a homemade book with photos of children in a key work group linked to 'Brown Bear Brown Bear, What Do You See?'

Aim: promoting the children's sense of belonging by developing a book about themselves

Resources: Published book, magnet board (metal sheets can be purchased cheaply at large DIY supermarkets – they need to be taped round the sharp edges), illustrations from the book preferably laminated and with magnetic strip on the back (rolls of magnetic strip can be purchased through educational catalogues), folder, plastic pockets and photographs of the children taken with parents permission on the home visit

FIGURE 9.19 *Keyworker shares with the group the Title and Author/Illustrator of the published book and the keywork group book they have made together. The children are familiar with the story and have had lots of opportunity to sequence it themselves using the pictures and the magnet board.*

FIGURE 9.20 *'Max, Max What do you see?'*

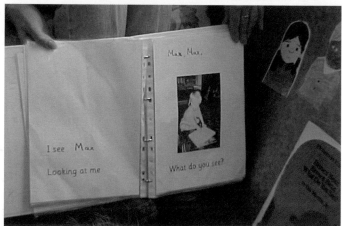

FIGURE 9.21 *'I see Preksha looking at me.'*

Learning opportunities linked to the Early Learning Goals

This activity provides opportunities for:

- **Personal, Social and Emotional Development**

  developing a sense of community and belonging to the group.

  supporting the development of confidence and willingness to be the focus of attention

  emotional satisfaction/pleasure in the use of the photographs of themselves

  turn taking and awareness of others through learning their names and identifying each other

- **Communication, Language and Literacy**

  joining in the familiar repeated phrases helps children to speak confidently and clearly

  awareness of how a book works and is put together

  print awareness starting with their names and the letters it is made up from and extended by the names of the other children in the group

- **Mathematical Development.**

  sequence and pattern in the order of the books

  matching the pictures and words to the books and opportunities for counting.

- **Knowledge and Understanding of the World**

  book making

  developing an interest in photographs and cameras

■ ROLE OF THE SUPPORTING ADULT

- to plan ahead to make the book by taking photographs on home visit and to compile the book with the children
- to introduce the keywork group book individually and in the group setting
- to make links between the storybook and the children's book
- responding to individual children and encouraging responses from quiet children
- developing storytelling
- supporting literacy links through children's names, their knowledge of the letters, noticing similarities in print through repeated phrases.

■ EXTENDING

- children making links with their own folders of photos and work and making their own books
- making links to other book formats such as zig zag books, flap books, peep hole books
- encouraging mark making, drawing and writing – a developmentally appropriate approach where adults can act as scribe, model writing and children confidently make marks to represent writing which progresses over time into conventional script
- using photographs to make books about other shared activities such as visits (if

possible using a digital camera where the children can see the pictures on the screen and help to decide which ones to print out on the computer – an excellent investment for any early years setting and these photographs form the basis of this book you are reading!)

■ HOME LINKS

■ encouraging parents/carers to share the keywork group book – for working parents it may be possible to send home for a night or so
■ encouraging families to make books about themselves and previous generations
■ supporting use of magnetic pictures and books with a lending library
■ making books about the local community

CHAPTER THREE *Activity*

Opportunities for mark making

Aim: To give children need oppotunities for making marks in a real and purposeful way during their play.

Resources: Resources need to be presented attractively and sorted on a regular basis. A pot of dried up felt pens without lids, broken or blunt pencils and scruffy paper will be unlikely to inspire children to experiment. Resources that are useful include:

A variety of writing tools – pencils, felt pens, crayons, coloured pencils, chalk, biros etc.

Different kinds of paper and card, forms, tickets, sticky labels, diaries, notebooks, clipboards, index books/cards, carbon paper, calendars and envelopes – all in various sizes/colours.

Such resources should be available in various areas of the settings both inside and out and can also be incorporated into role play areas such as, office, shop dentist, garage etc.

FIGURE 9.23 *Sam is writing her name on her painting so that everyone knows it belongs to her. She is able to form the letters competently.*

FIGURE 9.22 *Mummy Bear has telephoned Danielle to ask her to get some shopping for Baby Bear's Birthday. Danielle is writing a shopping list and making suggestions for what to buy. You need chocolate biscuits and cake. She is making letter like shapes confidently and is feeling what it is like to be a writer.*

FIGURE 9.24 *Leanne is writing a receipt in the shop.*

FIGURE 9.25 *Lauren is writing the price of the toys in the toyshop on sticky labels.*

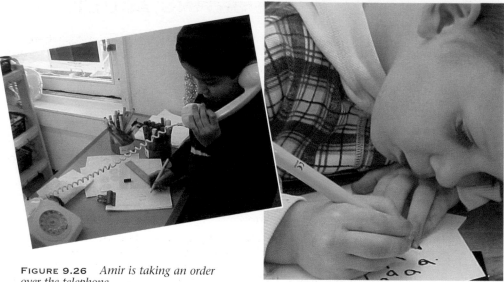

FIGURE 9.26   *Amir is taking an order over the telephone*

FIGURE 9.27   *Kealon is making a card. 'This is for my mummy, it says "I love you."' He is concentrating well and is using letter shapes that are familiar to him.*

Learning opportunities linked to the Early Learning Goals

This activity provides opportunities for:

- **Personal, Social and Emotional Development**

  developing confidence and a sense of achievement

  being able to join in with others,

  motivation to participate – involvement and concentration

- **Communication, Language and Literacy**

  holding a pencil effectively and developing confidence to explore mark making

  beginning to know their name, recognise it and attempt to write it

  being confident to make marks in a variety of situations

  beginning to understand that print in English goes from left to right

- **Mathematical Development**

  writing numerals on price tickets and receipts

- **Knowledge and Understanding of the World**

  selecting appropriate mark making tools for the task

  awareness of cultural scripts such as Chinese,Gujerati, Gaelic, Arabic

  mark making using different media such as paint, sand, clay, plasticine

  making marks on different surfaces such as: chalkboards, tiles, magic slates, computers, acetate, paper and card of different textures,and learning about their different properties

- **Physical Development**

  handling tools and developing small manipulative movements

  increasing co-ordination, deciding hand preference and developing an effective pencil grip

- **Creative Development**

  experimental marks leading to creative drawing and writing

■ ROLE OF THE SUPPORTING ADULT

- ■ to provide quality resources and plan a range of purposeful experiences where children feel in control
- ■ to invite and find ways of interesting children in participating without compelling them
- ■ to model writing for children and act as a scribe for them
- ■ to have a range of print around the setting that the children can see, use and respond to
- ■ to observe and get to know individual children and their level of skill in order to build on this in a sensitive and supportive way
- ■ to respect children's early marks, to accept them as a real contribution and to build on this.

The practice of tracing or copying letters and using work sheets is not meaningful for very young children. They need to write for a purpose and to feel free to experiment and have a go. As a compulsory activity it is unlikely to motivate children and may even deter them. Children who do not feel confident to reproduce the letters correctly often refuse and say 'I can't do that'.

■ EXTENDING

- ■ tuning into children's interests and finding ways of making marks that link with these
- ■ as children are ready to link sounds to letters and words enabling them to attempt writing simple words
- ■ sharing approaches to mark making with parents and carers emphasising the importance of developing confidence in the children and accepting and respecting their early attempts
- ■ respecting, sharing and displaying the additional languages of families so extending the knowledge of all those in the setting.

Equal opportunities – access to the learning

- ■ Visual props should be used to enhance understanding for all children.
- ■ Stories should reflect the diversity of different cultures and family life. They should challenge stereotypical portrayal of gender, culture and disability.

- ■ Dual text books, including those in Braille, accustom children to different language styles and stress their value.
- ■ Noise level in the setting should be a level which enables children to hear and be heard.

Health and safety

- Care must be taken that children do not put small props or pen tops in their mouths.
- Non-toxic writing materials should be used.
- Children should be discouraged from walking around with pencils.

Further reading, information and sources

Books and Stories (1994) Play Activities Series, Pre-school Learning Alliance.

Yates, I. *Language and Literacy*. Scholastic.

Whitehead, M. (1996) *The Development of Language and Literacy*. London: Hodder and Stoughton.

Gussin Paley, V. (1990) *The Boy Who Would be a Helicopter – the use of storytelling in the classroom*. Harvard University Press.

Sharing stories and making marks NVQ links

Level 2
C 1.4, C 4, C 8.1, C 8.4, C 8.5, C 9.2, C 9.4, C 9.5, P 1.1
Level 3
C 2.4, C 3.4, C 5, C 10, C 11, C 15.4, M 7, P 2.3

10

Music and Movement

Music and movement are expressive arts through which children can communicate and share their feelings. They are pleasurable experiences building on children's natural responses to sound. Moving to music helps children become more aware of their bodies. They learn how it moves and flows as their control develops.

Singing and making music enables all children to communicate freely by giving them other ways to express themselves. The rhythm and repetition supports speech and language development. It builds up children's confidence both while participating as part of a group and exploring on their own or in pairs.

Children learn to appreciate these experiences and playing music from different home cultures forms important links. Music can evoke a diversity of emotional responses and visual images can be associated with the sounds. The emotional tone of music can enable children to talk about their feelings and what is happening.

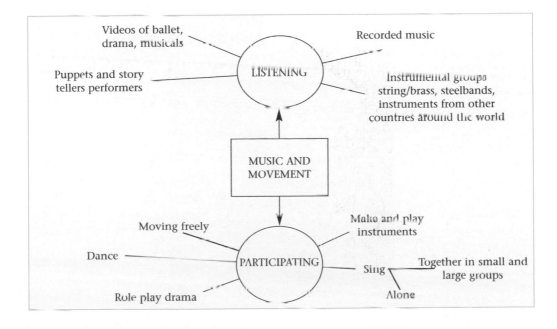

CHAPTER TEN *Activity*

Playing up and down the scale on xylophones and glockenspiel

Aim: to encourage children through story to explore the varying pitches and notes in a musical scale

Resources: A xylophone (wooden) or glockenspiel (metallic) with beaters rubber or wooden

Stories involving stairs or ladders – playpeople and fire engines and ladders

(with the flat xylophone need to prop up safely against a wall to help develop the concept of up and down)

FIGURES 10.1, 10.2
The adult is reading and telling a story about a family who are climbing up and falling down stairs. While she tells the story the children perform the actions with playpeople or the beaters. They then enjoy making their own up and down stories

FIGURE 10.3 *Joe is making the fire-fighter climb up the ladder as Amber plays up the notes of the scale on the xylophone*

Learning opportunities linked to the Early Learning Goals

This activity provides opportunities for:

- **Personal, Social and Emotional Development**

  taking turns and being part of a small group

  gaining confidence to try new activities

  expressing emotions through sounds and story

- **Communication, Language and Literacy**

  acquiring new vocabulary

  using prepositions and positional language

- **Mathematical Development**

  for using comparative language for example high and low

  creating and repeating patterns

- **Knowledge and Understanding of the World**

  exploring and experimenting with sound that the instruments make

  experience volume and vibration and to discriminate between sounds

  questioning why the sounds change and what is happening

- **Physical Development**

  developing hand-eye co-ordination

  developing fine motor control in handling the beaters and small figures

- **Creative Development**

  expressing ideas and feelings through sound

■ ROLE OF THE ADULT

- to set up the instruments and involve the children through story and props
- to ensure all the children get the opportunity to listen and participate
- to encourage them to recognise the high and low sounds and how they come together in a scale
- to encourage use of descriptive language
- to involve the children's ideas.

■ EXTENDING

- providing opportunities for children to experiment freely and develop their own ideas
- making musical instruments which make different sounds
- looking at vibrations and how sound travels (two empty tins joined with a taut piece of string for children to speak messages to each other)
- developing other aspects of music such as loud/soft, fast/slow
- developing a sound lotto or sound recognition memory game using different pitches or sounds
- using other instruments to explore these musical ideas for example stringed instruments for vibrations
- involving music and story together – traditional tales and rhymes – using instruments to represent characters and effects.

■ HOME LINKS

- encouraging parents/carers to join music making sessions in the setting and to make music at home
- making tapes for listening in the setting and at home
- sharing adult's skills in playing instruments
- involve community groups and school musicians to perform for the children.

CHAPTER TEN *Activity*

Learning about ballet from a ballerina

Aim: To extend children's experience of a form of dance and to participate in a movement session

Resources: Large space, a skilled adult, dance equipment, music

FIGURES 10.4, 10.5, 10.6 *The children were invited to join the small group. They didn't have to remove their shoes if the didn't want to and they could leave when they wanted. Kathryn shared with the children her interest and expertise in ballet. She brought in tutus, ballet shoes and music. She demonstrated some basic ballet steps and then invited the children to join in a movement session with her.*

Learning opportunities linked to the Early Learning Goals

This activity provides opportunities for:

- **Personal, Social and Emotional Development**

  being involved as part of a group

  developing their confidence to join in with a new activity

  developing self-help skills in managing their clothes

  opportunities for concentration and engagement

- **Communication, Language and Literacy**

  listening and responding to the experience

  acquiring new vocabulary

  developing other means of expression such as movement and gesture, which all children can access irrespective of their spoken language competence

- **Mathematical Development**

  opportunities to match, copy and follow a pattern of movement

- **Knowledge and Understanding of the world**

  experiencing one aspect of dance

- **Physical Development**

  developing body awareness and co-ordination.

  experiencing themselves and others moving in space

  developing fine motor skills through managing their clothes

- **Creative Development**

  expressing themselves through movement and responding to music

■ ROLE OF THE SUPPORTING ADULT

- to provide a suitably sized space – free from distractions or interruptions
- to involve, motivate and sustain the interest of the children.
- to share their knowledge and skills, but also to be responsive to the children's contributions.

■ EXTENDING

- exploring a wide range of body movements and encouraging self expression
- responding to a variety of musical styles and integrating with other media such as paint, fabric, ribbons
- introducing different kinds of dance e.g.: folk dancing, Indian dancing, tap dancing, maypole dancing, Irish dancing, Latin American dancing, line dancing including costume and props
- creating opportunities for children to be part of an audience.

■ HOME LINKS

- encouraging adults in the community to come and share their skills
- creating opportunities for adults to join in with their children's experiences – in school, in the home and during weekend groups.

CHAPTER TEN *Activity*

Singing together

Aim: to engage children in a musical activity together with others

Resources: Appropriate space for the size of the group

Adults to plan, lead and support the music making – a guitar is an excellent instrument to accompany young children's singing. The player is on the children's level, facing them and the guitar is soft and melodious. Sometimes it is a good idea if the children become familiar with the songs in smaller groups. Songs can be tape-recorded (children and/or adults singing and playing) and available at different times to individuals and small groups.

FIGURE 10.7   *5 Firefighters standing in a row*
1,2,3,4,.....WOOSH they go
One jumped off the engine with a 'shout' – FIRE
Quicker than a wink the fire went out
1,2,3   WOOSH WOOSH they go
1,2   WOOSH WOOSH WOOSH they go
1   WOOSH WOOSH WOOSH WOOSH they go
Standing all alone WOOSH WOOSH WOOSH WOOSH WOOSH he/she goes

Learning opportunities linked to the Early Learning Goals

This activity provides opportuntles for:

- **Personal, Social and Emotional Development**

  enjoying being part of a large group – listening to others and taking turns

  experiencing satisfaction in making a contribution and a sense of well-being

  gaining the confidence to volunteer and take part

- **Communication, Language and Literacy**

  repetition, rhythm and rhyme supporting development of speech

  using and extending vocabulary

  listening to onset (see Glossary) and rime

  increasing auditory memory and making links with other speech and language

- **Mathematical Development**

  recognising and becoming familiar with

  practising counting – ordinal and cardinal – adding to and taking away from (mental mathematics)

- **Knowledge and Understanding of the World**

  Experience songs from different cultures

- **Physical Development**

  developing muscle tone and breathing co-ordination

  using voice with range, pitch and rhythm

- **Creative Development**

  building a repertoire of songs and rhymes

■ ROLE OF THE ADULT

- to plan, lead and involve the children in the group singing
- to model music making and introduce a wide range of songs and rhymes
- to ensure all the group benefits by supporting children's confidence in taking turns to contribute.

■ EXTENDING

- Personalising songs and adapting words (Johnny, Johnny how are you today?)
- using the songs to extend current themes and interest in the setting
- making links with stories (Noah, Three Bears) and events (Chinese Dragon, Father Christmas) or visits (I went to visit the farm one day)
- taping songs so children can use independently
- using and making musical instruments to accompanying singing and music sessions
- on occasions inviting an audience or others to share the experience
- introducing examples of musical notation and encouraging notation mark making
- making links with sound recognition and lotto games
- encouraging children to compose and sing their own songs.

■ HOME LINKS

- sharing the words of the songs (photocopied sheets) to encourage parents to sing with the children at home
- making tapes they can take home and play
- inviting parents in to listen and to share some songs they know or to play an accompanying instrument
- sharing cultural celebrations and traditional songs at home and bringing into school

Equal opportunities – access to the learning

- Provide a range of instruments and songs from different cultures.
- Use instruments which vibrate to stimulate children with hearing impairment.
- Instruments can be suspended so that they can be hit with one hand.
- Beware of stereotypical song and rhymes.
- Children with behavioural difficulties can respond to calming music.

Health and safety

- Area for movement should be safe and cleared of hazards.
- Any home-made instruments, e.g. shakers made with uncooked pulses should be supervised carefully during making and playing.

Further reading, information and sources

Henderson, A. (1993) *Music through Play*. Learn through Play Series, Pre-school Learning Alliance.

Pegg, L. (1997) *Learning through Music*. Leamington Spa: Scholastic.

Harrison, L. (1998) *Learning through Dance and Drama*. Leamington Spa: Scholastic.

Harrop B., Friend L. and Gadsby D. (1995) *Okki-tokki-unga*. London: A&C Black.

Harriet Powell (1983) *Game Songs with Prof Dogg's Troupe*. London: A&C Black.

Music and movement NVQ links

Level 2Level 2

C 1.3, C 4.2, C 4.3, C 4.4, C4.5, C 9.1, C 9.2, C 9.3, C 9.5, E 1.1, E 2.2, M 3.1

Level 3

C 3, C 5.2, C 5.3, C 5.4, C 5.5, C 7.3, C 10, C 11, M 7, P 2.3

Games and Puzzles

Completing puzzles and participating in games provide opportunities for children to play both alone and in a group, with or without an adult. There is a wide range of such activities which provide both a challenge and satisfaction to the pre-school child and encourage concentration and perseverance.

Both table and ring games involve learning rules and encourage turn-taking and sharing. They bring with them the difficult lesson that the child might not always win. Play with puzzles, although generally a more solitary task, does involve some cooperation among children as they select, manipulate, sort and match pieces.

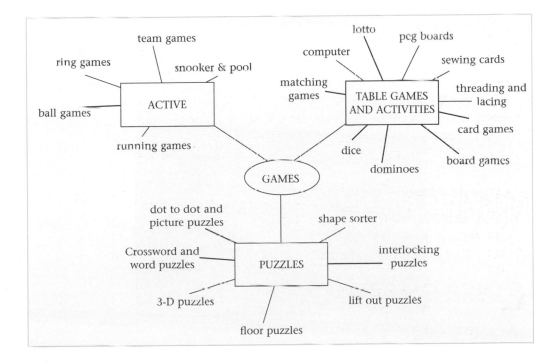

CHAPTER ELEVEN *Activity*

Snail Game

Aim: to play a game in a small group

Resources: Snail game, suitable floor space or table

The snail game offers non competitive opportunities for taking turns. The children throw coloured dice and move the corresponding snail. It is the snail that wins, not the child. This game can be played by an individual child or in varying size groups.

FIGURES 11.1, 11.2 *William said: 'It's your turn to throw the dice Alcin', 'It's yellow, I'll move the yellow snail, now it's Kanji's turn.'*

FIGURE 11.3 *WILLIAM: 'The white one has finished' 'The blue one is last'*

Learning opportunities linked to the Early Learning Goals

This activity provides opportunities for:

- **Personal, Social and Emotional Development**

  developing concentration skills

  learning to take turns and enjoy working as part of a group

  learning that games have rules

  developing confidence to try new activities and experiences

- **Communication, Language and Literacy**

  describing action and verbalising rules

- **Mathematical Development**

  matching colours

  using ordinal and cardinal number

  using mathematical language to indicate direction

  developing mathematical concepts, e.g. only one more; five have finished; one more to go; which one do you think will finish first?

- **Knowledge and Understanding of the World**

  making links with the outside environment

- **Physical Development**

  developing hand-eye co-ordination

■ ROLE OF THE SUPPORTING ADULT

- to introduce the rules of the game, encouraging them to take turns and match the dice
- to develop the appropriate language
- to encourage children to talk about their experiences.

■ EXTENDING

- making up new rules for this game
- using as part of a mini beasts theme
- taking children on a nature walk and snail hunt
- looking at patterns and spirals
- drawing maps and enhancing links with directional awareness
- making their own snails out of salt dough, bake them and paint them making links with cooking activities – spiral sandwiches, yeast extract whirls, spiral patterns on biscuits
- introduce other games also with rules e.g.:
  - card games (snap, happy families)
  - matching (lotto, dominoes)
  - memory games (Kim's Game, pelmanism)
  - constructional (games building up a picture)
  - using computer games
- making up own games.

■ HOME LINKS

- ■ encourage parents to play games with the children and have fun by welcoming them to into the setting, sharing photographs of these activities and by lending out resources
- ■ encourage children to bring in games from home.

CHAPTER ELEVEN *Activity*

Ring game

Aim: to encourage children to have the confidence to participate in a ring game

Resources: Enough space to make a circle of seated children and for running around the outside, something to lie on if necessary, a pretend pot of honey

FIGURES 11.4, 11.5   *ISN'T IT FUNNY HOW A BEAR LIKES HONEY*
BUZZ BUZZ BUZZ I WONDER WHY HE DOES
GO TO SLEEP MRS BEAR
Adult chooses a child to tiptoe in and take the honey pot.
WAKE UP MRS BEAR YOUR HONEY'S NOT THERE
Mrs Bear jumps up and chases after the child with her honey.
This child goes around the outside of the circle and brings the pot back into the centre.

Learning opportunities linked to the Early Learning Goals

This activity provides opportunities for:

- **Personal, Social and Emotional Development**

  generating interest and excitement

  helping all children to participate confidently in the game

  co-operating as part of a group

- **Communication, Language and Literacy**

  listening with enjoyment and following instructions in a story sequence of events

  promoting language develoment through the use of rhyme and repetition

- **Mathematical Development**

  promoting spatial awareness

  following a repeating pattern

- **Physical Development**

  developing co-ordination and control

- **Creative Development**

  deep involvement in an imaginative game

■ ROLE OF THE SUPPORTING ADULT

- to invite children to participate and teach them the rhyme and sequence of events
- to play the game with the children, making sure everyone is listening, the bear goes to sleep, choose the child to take the honey and ensure safety
- support shy children to feel confident to have a turn, and join in when they are ready.

■ EXTENDING

- introducing other ring games, Sandy Girl/Boy, There was a Princess Long Ago, Farmer's in his Den, What's the Time Mr. Wolf
- making up own words or ring games using children's experience and ideas
- to link with action rhymes: Head shoulders knees and toes, I'm a dinosaur, 5 currant buns, speckled frogs
- to encourage children to play games themselves.

■ HOME LINKS

- encouraging parents/carers to play the games at home and other settings by making tape recordings and booklets
- inviting parents/carers and others in the community to bring in their rhymes and games.

CHAPTER ELEVEN *Activity*

Floor puzzle

Aim: to provide the opportunity for children to co-operate together in completing a picture

Resources: Adequate, clean floor space, a variety of large puzzles

FIGURE 11.6 *Jack, David and Roselyn are helped by Emma to complete a train number puzzle*

Learning opportunities linked to the Early Learning Goals

This activity provides opportunities for:

- **Personal, Social and Emotional Development**

  cooperating as part of a small group

  taking turns

  developing concentration, perseverence and patience

- **Communication, Language and Literacy**

  talking about the pictures

  differentiating between letter and number symbols

- **Mathematical Development**

  recognition of number symbols

  counting up to 10 and completing a number sequence

  recognition of pattern and shape

  problem solving and estimating, promoting logical thought

- **Knowledge and Understanding of the World**

  exploring similarities and differences in pattern

  using trial and error, gradually developing strategies to fit pieces together to achieve an end product

- **Physical Development**

  development of hand-eye coordination

- **Creative Development**

  exploration of colour and shape

  aesthetic awareness

■ ROLE OF THE SUPPORTING ADULT

- to encourage thought and prompt where appropriate
- to ensure children take turns and support them where necessary.

■ EXTENDING

- puzzles with more pieces
- puzzles with larger numbers or alphabet symbols
- completing puzzles independently
- make their own puzzles.

■ HOME LINKS

- encourage parents/carers to do puzzles with their children
- borrow puzzles from a toy library.

Equal opportunities – access to the learning

- All children should be encouraged to participate.
- Puzzles should include non-stereotypical images of gender, disability and culture.
- Allow children to select their own games and puzzles.
- Have puzzles with large knobs for children who may have special needs.
- Games and puzzles with different textures and raised features enable the participation of children with visual impairment.

Health and safety

- A safe, clean area without hazards is needed for ring games and floor puzzles.
- Care should be taken that children do not put small playing pieces in their mouths, noses and ears.

Further reading, information and sources

Taverner, J. (1998) *Learning through Table-top Games*. Leamington Spa: Scholastic.

Games and puzzles NVQ links

Level 2
C 1.3, C 1.4, C 4.2, C 4.3, C 4.5, C 8.2, C 8.4, C 9.2, E 2.1, E 2.2, P 1.1
Level 3
C 2.4, C 3, C 5.2, C 5.3, C 5.5, C 7.1, C 7.2, C 10.1, C 10.2, C 10.3, C 11.1, C 11.2, C 11.4, C 11.5, C 15.4, M 7, P 2.3

12

Information and Communication Technology (ICT)

Children will bring into the early years setting very different knowledge and understanding of ICT. They will all need to acquire skills to allow them to access this technology which is everywhere in our lives. Children find technology exciting and motivating. They quickly learn how to operate buttons and key pads and mouse and directional skills. Practitioners need to offer a range of opportunities to use technology in the setting, to observe children's skills and offer support to enable each individual child to use ICT confidently and competently. Access to information should not just be a solitary activity but should be shared in small groups and enrich the whole curriculum. Watching others, sharing your skills with others and working together with the information.

Personal computers have enabled great access to information at many levels. A greater range of affordable and relevant software is now available. It is important, however, for practitioners to view before purchase as some programmes are very poor, just repetitive rote learning with unacceptable elements of violence and stereotypical scenarios. Some so called 'educational' toys are also very often limited. Access to the internet can now also be obtained through games consoles. Children's' homes also have many technological sources of information and communication such as televisions, videos, telephones, cameras, game consoles, calculators, electronic musical instruments, stereos, CD players, DVD players and tape recorders. This is an important area to link learning for all the family so that adults and children gain confident access to this technology.

INFORMATION	COMMUNICATION	TECHNOLOGY
Stories, music, reference information presented for young children		Audio and video tape recorder
		Stills cameras – film and digital
	Storing	
Photographs of people and world around children Numerical data	Accessing	Calculators
	Using	Programmable toys, games, consoles
Simple programming i.e. directions and actions	Sharing	
	Knowledge	Telephones, answering machine
Voice communication		Faxes Photocopier Personal computer
Written/pictorial information		Internet and electronic mail

CHAPTER TWELVE *Activity*

Using tape recorders

Aim: To enable children to use technology to independently access stories and music

Resources: It is best to use a high quality tape recorder especially designed for educational use. The tape recorder in our picture has the facility to take up to 5 headsets (one is a master socket which cuts out the speakers), parts can be replaced and the machine maintained. Children can listen with or without headsets and control the volume for themselves. Comfortable quiet seating area. Sets of the same story book enable each child can have their own copy or they can one book and any accompanying props.

FIGURE 12.1 *Billy has elected to control the tape recorder for the group. He is experimenting with the volume control. Once he has wound the story back to the beginning he and Adam will begin reading their books again.*

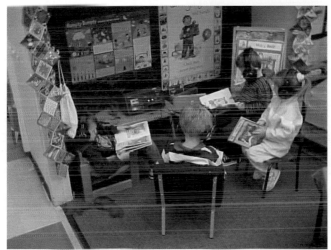

FIGURE 12.2 *The tape recorder has 5 jack sockets so that each child has their own headphones. This enables them to sit comfortably and to enjoy the story individually.*

FIGURE 12.3 *The tape recorder was set up in the nursery garden to give those children who spend a lot of time outside the opportunity to hear and participate in stories.*

Learning opportunities linked to the Early Learning Goals

This activity provides opportunities for:

- **Personal, Social and Emotional Development**

  developing and extending concentration

  sharing a relaxed social experience

- **Communication, Language and Literacy**

  enjoying listening and responding to stories, knowledge of how story books work

  sequencing stories, retelling narratives, using story props and making up their own

  sustaining attentive listening

- **Mathematical Development**

  offering stories with a mathematical content

- **Knowledge and Understanding of the World**

  finding out about how tape recorders work, switching on and off, rewinding and turning tapes over and learning about everyday technology

- **Physical Development**

  using small equipment with increasing control

- **Creative Development**

  adding to their rich experience of stories and the world of imagination

■ ROLE OF THE SUPPORTING ADULT

- to ensure the equipment is safe and in good repair
- to show children how to use it safely and how to adjust the volume so that it does not harm their hearing
- to demonstrate how to use the controls on the tape recorder
- to assist the children to adjust and put the ear phones on
- to listen along with the children initially to model where the story begins and how to use the picture clues to turn the pages as the story progresses.

■ EXTENDING

- recording stories with the children
- recording sound effect tapes for games such as sound lotto
- offering tapes of music, rhymes and songs from different cultures
- offering tapes of different types of music opera, classical music, jazz, folk, rock and popular music
- visiting a music studio
- following up in a group session using a big book version.

■ HOME AND COMMUNITY LINKS

- build up a tape lending library – including copies of the book and story props

- encourage bi-lingual families to record well known stories and stories from their own cultures for use in the setting and in the lending library
- encourage families to listen together and share the experience of the stories
- suggest making other sound recordings at home and in the locality
- extend to using cameras to record pictorially.

CHAPTER TWELVE *Activity*

Using calculators in pretend play

Aim: To provide opportunities to operate calculators and extend their knowledge of numbers

Resources: Several sturdy calculators, till and money, simple set of balance scales, things to buy and sell, paper and pencils, paper and stapler to make bags and wrap parcels

FIGURE 12.4 *Lauren is using the calculator to add up the shopping that Preksha and Callum have bought. She fills the screen with numbers, clears them and then taps in some more. She makes a list of fruit and vegetables using letters from her name, numbers and marks*

FIGURE 12.5 *Preksha, inspired by Lauren's use of the calculator takes over as the shopkeeper. She finds numbers on the calculator that are the same as on the till and presses them both.*

Learning opportunities linked to the Early Learning Goals

This activity provides opportunities for:

- **Personal, Social and Emotional Development**

  responding and interacting as part of group play

  sharing equipment and respecting others ideas and to take turns

- **Communication, Language and Literacy**

  writing for a purpose and using a pencil or pen

  interacting with peers imaginatively

  writing lists using marks, numerals, letters and words

- **Mathematical Development**

  saying and using numbers in familiar contexts, to recognise numerals, to compare quantities, using language 'more', 'less', 'heavy', 'light'

- **Knowledge and Understanding of the World**

  finding out about everyday technology

  experiencing cause and effect by making links between pressing the number button and it appearing on the display

- **Physical Development**

  to increase control and co-ordination through manipulation of buttons

- **Creative Development**

  using their imagination

  developing and extending social communication through role play

■ ROLE OF THE SUPPORTING ADULT

- to observe the children's level of knowledge and support their use and understanding of calculator
- to set up the role play attractively to encourage children to use it
- to sensitively intervene in a subordinate role to support and extend the interaction, language and use of equipment.

■ EXTENDING

- making links with first hand experiences – visits to a variety of shops
- singing number rhymes using cards to show the numbers visually to complement the experience and understanding of number
- providing calculators in other role play scenarios such as offices, other shops such as DIY, hairdresser, post office
- providing calculators for everyday use in the writing, mathematics and other areas of provision to encourage usage and familiarity through self choice.

■ HOME LINKS

- to involve parents and encourage them to share with the children their use of calculators at home and at work
- to involve the children in the many number opportunities in everyday life

including when visiting shops, paying bills and working out costs of say an outing

■ to include calculators in a sharing library for home use.

CHAPTER TWELVE *Activity*

Using a computer

Aim: to give children experience with computers and to learn to operate the controls to enable them to independently access and use the programmes.

Resources: A computer with input device such as keyboard or mouse (this needs to be at a level accessible for children – a low table with blocks if needed is more flexible than standard computer trolleys). A range of computer programs which are age appropriate. A printer allows a hard copy of text and some pictures so that the child can share with others their learning and the processes. Sand timers to regulate turn taking. Paper and pens for children to record whose turn is next. Seating and agreed procedures for group use.

FIGURE 12.6   *SHEILAGH: 'Callum has written his name and it is his turn after James. Would you like to write your name Robert so we can remember that your turn is after Callum?'*
ROBERT: 'R for Robert . . .'.

Learning opportunities linked to the Early Learning Goals

This activity provides opportunities for:

■ **Personal, Social and Emotional Development**

developing and extending concentration and focusing on the elements of the programs

developing independence and the confidence in their ability to make choices and decisions.

working alongside and with small groups – taking turns – learning through observation and engagement

■ **Communication, Language and Literacy**

enabling work with pictures, symbols, numbers, sounds, words, text at differentiated levels with opportunities for self correction and support through the learning programs

■ **Mathematical Development**

accessing a range of programs to develop skills in matching, sorting, number concepts and sets

■ **Knowledge and Understanding of the World**

accessing information and using images and sound in many areas of learning

understanding cause and effect through use of input devices changing images on the screen

■ **Physical Development**

developing co-ordination and using fine motor control

■ **Creative Development**

working creatively with colour and images in 2 and 3 dimensions through programs

■ ROLE OF THE SUPPORTING ADULT

■ to be familiar and competent with the technology
■ to carefully view and select programs that are suitable for their children
■ to plan time to show children how to access the computer programs independently
■ to observe the child's level of skill and support where appropriate
■ to share their involvement and support by commenting on what is happening
■ to extend their vocabulary including technical terms such as *mouse, menu, load, print, exit.*

■ EXTENDING

■ reinforce the learning offered in the computer programs in other activities within the setting
■ link programs with topics or themes as possible
■ set up role play areas such as offices with computer to extend their familiarisation with keyboards
■ familiarise children with the use of computers in everyday life for example shops, offices, banks
■ using other programmable toys.

■ HOME LINKS

■ informing parents/carers about the sorts of programs the children are using, encouraging them to come and use the material themselves with the children and encouraging them to let the setting know about skills and programs they are using at home

■ encouraging families to use local facilities such as schools, colleges and libraries which access to training, borrowing programs and hands on use of computers.

Equal opportunities – access to the learning

■ Ensure all children have access to computerised equipment.

■ Specialised computerised equipment can support communication and learning for children with special needs – these may be loaned or hired from central services.

■ Sight impaired children will need a larger font.

■ For children with language and communication difficulties, computers can be an excellent support.

■ Use story tapes in a variety of languages.

■ Technology should be available in all areas of provision, e.g. Calculators, telephones in role play, tape recorders in creative areas.

Health and safety

■ Children should be shown how to use the equipment safely.

■ All electrical equipment must be checked on a regular basis. Unused sockets should be protected with covers (dummy plugs).

■ Children should not be allowed to remove batteries or plugs.

■ Volume control should be monitored carefully so as not to harm hearing.

■ Children should not be allowed to move heavy equipment, which should be sited where it cannot be knocked and so fall.

Further reading, information and sources

Henderson, A. (1992) *Technology through Play*. Learn through Play Series, Pre-school Learning Alliance.

Information communication technology NVQ links

Level 2

C 1.4, C 4.2, C 4.3, C 4.5, C 8.2, C 8.4, C 9.2, C 9.3, C 9.5, E 2.1, E 2.2, M 3.1, P 1.1

Level 3

C 2.4, C 3.4, C 5.2, C 5.3, C 7.1, C 10.1, C 10.2, C 10.3, C 11.2, C 11.3, C 11.5, M 7, P 2.3

13

Babies and Toddlers

Babies learn while still in their mother's womb. From birth they use all their senses to find out all about what surrounds them. Recent research has produced evidence to confirm the immense importance of early stimulus with babies. (Trevarthan 1993). As well as their basic needs for food, warmth and care, babies need significant people to relate to and interact with who will help them develop.

Babies respond to faces and close physical contact. All the physical care routines such as changing nappies, bathing and mealtimes, are important times for the adult to interact with their baby. 'Bath your baby in language' (Bullock Report, 1975). Very young babies will hold turn taking conversations with their carer and respond actively to the speech sounds and tone of voice. There is a magnetism about babies that makes many people want to respond to them.

Sometimes babies and toddlers do become frustrated and bad tempered. It is important to acknowledge this and incorporate techniques to distract or comfort them. Children often have to protest, it is part of their learning to cope. Adults have to survive this and try to channel energies into positive activities. Sharing, turn taking and negotiating need to be modelled by adults and consistently encouraged in the babies and toddlers as they mature.

Times set aside for adults to play with and respond to the baby are also important to plan for. Although a very young baby needs the security of carers they know, as they become more experienced in other settings they are enabled to explore wider relationships at appropriate stages. Babies enjoy being part of family activities and will benefit from watching as well as being involved.

The photographs in this chapter were taken in the Family Room provision at our nursery school. We hold two daily drop-in play sessions where parents and carers stay and play with their babies and toddlers. Two staff welcome and register the families. They offer support and a range of activities. Health professionals recommend the provision to families. A range of support activities is offered to parents and carers Parenting Programmes, Family Literacy, OU Course 'Confident Parents Confident Children', Communication Workshops, Problem Solving Approaches to Conflict.

■ HOW BABIES LEARN

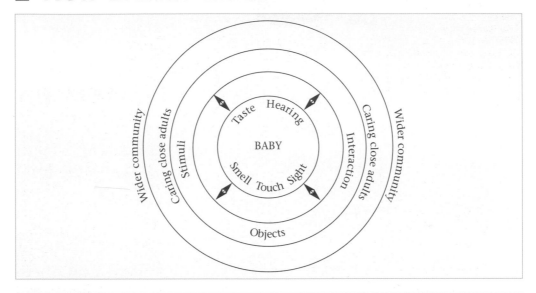

CHAPTER THIRTEEN *Activity*

Singing songs and having a conversation together

Samuel is 5 and a half months old. His mother brings him weekly to the Family Room. She enjoys contact with other parents. Samuel loves to watch everything around him and particularly loves the singing together that the session ends with

FIGURES 13.1, 13.2, 13.3, 13.4, 13.5
Row, row, row your boat gently down the stream
Merrily, merrily, merrily, merrily, life is but a dream
Are you enjoying that?
It's good fun

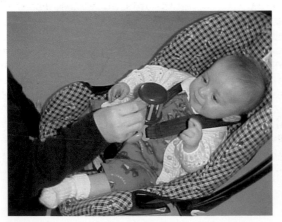

More?
Who's a beautiful boy?
Samuel? Yes you.
We like this don't we.
What have I got?
Can you hear the bell? What's that:
Ding, ding ding ding
You want to hold it?
We've got one of these at home
Shake it
Yes, that it

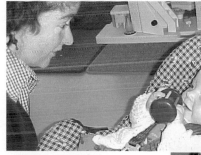

FIGURE 13.6 *End of session singing*

CHAPTER THIRTEEN *Activity*

Exploring with wooden spoons and pots

Everyday and natural objects give babies many exciting opportunities to use all their senses to actively explore. They find out about the different properties of the materials and how they can be used and manipulated. Very young babies will explore with their mouths, especially if their gums are irritated through teething. They like to move the object around in space and love to hear the sounds as they bang them together.

Before babies are independently mobile adults and older children need to ensure that they can reach objects and explore safely. They need to stay nearby the baby so that support can be quickly offered and too much frustration avoided. Babies enjoy the company of other babies as well as older people and love to watch and make contact.

Elinor Goldschmeid (1992) promoted her idea of a 'treasure basket'. This is a collection of natural or man made objects which are safe stimulating for the child to explore, particularly before they are able to crawl.

FIGURE 13.7   *Rebecca is 7½ months old. She able to sit up unsupported for quite long periods and can reach for objects that attract her. She is teething and loves the feel of the wooden spoon in her mouth.*

FIGURES 13.8, 13.9, 13.10, 13.11   *Yaseen is 10½ months old and he is a physically active explorer. He enjoys the challenge of putting the lid on the pot and using the spoons as drumsticks. He stayed and played with these toys for around half an hour and only stopped as it was time to go.*

CHAPTER THREE *Activity*

Sensory fun together with cornflour

Cornflour is a fascinating and engaging material. Adults and children spend long periods handling the cornflour and talking together. It changes from a liquid, flowing state to a solid, malleable one in seconds. It is smooth and can be cold to touch or warmed by adding hot water. It can be coloured with food dyes. As it dries out children can add more water by using spray bottles and observe the changes. It is non-toxic and when it is spread everywhere is easily removed from objects, skin and clothing. A large shallow tray enables several families to play together. It should not be covered overnight but left open to the air. It usually last two or three days but needs careful monitoring for cleanliness.

FIGURE 13.12   *Leah is 8 months old. She is sitting on her mother's lap reaching out to catch the trickle of cornflour from the plastic scrapper. She is learning co-ordinate and control her hand-eye movements.*

FIGURE 13.13   *Fallon is 1 year old and is also sitting on her mother's lap. They are both enjoying the feel of the cornflour on their fingers. They also use the plastic scrapers to move it around the tray. Fallon spends lots of time watching Molly who is 2½. Molly regularly spends long periods exploring the cornflour and talks to Fallon about what she is doing.*

FIGURE 13.14   *Fallon is fascinated by the drips of cornflour as they trickles off her fingers.*

FIGURE 13.15   *Tom is 2½ years old and stands at the tray. His mother is seated close behind him and she comments on what he is doing. As well as using the sprayer to wet the cornflour Tom experiments with washing it off his hand.*

CHAPTER THIRTEEN *Activity*

Playing together with a wooden train set

Oliver is 23 months old and loves to play with trains. His mother sits close and watches. She listens to him and comments on what is happening. This promotes his language and social development. She is also able to maintain his play by helping when the long train collapses. After a time she suggests they look at a book together to extend his interest.

Oliver chose several board books about trains from the racks in the book corner of the Family Room.

FIGURES 13.16, 13.17, 13.18
'That's a very long train you've made.'
'Are you going to push or pull the engine?'
'Oh, you are pushing the train backwards.'
'Oops, it fell off the track.'
'Shall I help?'
'There, ready to go now'

CHAPTER THIRTEEN *Activity*

Playing together with a range of activities

Alex is 23 months old. His mum brings him to the Family Room regularly to give them time together without other children and family members. Alex is confident and makes many choices. He likes to try all the activities on offer and moves independently between them. His concentration is good and his mum extends this by her involvement.

FIGURES 13.19, 13.20   *As well as ample amount of dough there are also a range of cooking utensils and pots on the table. More equipment can be easily accessed from nearby storage. Alex's fine motor control is developing and he is knowledgeable about pans and cookers. Mum helps him roll the dough flat to enable him to cut out a cake to put in the oven. She talks with him about what they are doing.*

FIGURE 13.21   *Alex explores the range of musical instruments. He has just been lifted up by his mum to reach some wind chimes hanging nearby. He listens carefully and with enjoyment to the different sounds.*

FIGURES 13.22, 13.23, 13.24   *Alex grasps the chunky chalk in his right hand (he seems to be developing right hand dominance) and starts by making vertical lines. He reaches up and joins some of these and is very pleased with the end product.*

Equal opportunities – access to the learning

- The stated aim of the provision is for parents/carers to 'come in, relax and play with your child' and staff support the adults in this to ensure the involvement of all.
- It is a drop-in where all parents/carers are welcome and if the session is too full a reservation is made for another day for the family turned away.
- A range of materials are easily accessible in the Family playroom and parents/carers shown how to get more puzzles, books and other resources from the adjoining parent's room.

- The provision is carefully planned and staff can quickly obtain other activities and equipment from the nursery stocks to ensure suitability for the children attending the session.
- Parents/carers who attend regularly offer to help support activities and are involved in resourcing the provision to ensure it reflects the community around it.
- Parents/carers are given information to ensure they feel confident in using the provision and have access to the school management.

Health and safety

- Hygiene is especially important where young children are involved and the areas babies may lie or crawl on are disinfected daily. Also toys and objects babies and toddlers may put in their mouths must be similarly treated.
- Nappy changing area needs to be separate, disinfected regularly and disposable paper towel provided for use each time. Plastic nappy sacks and sealed plastic.

- bags/containers should be regularly disposed of.
- Need to ensure that areas accessed by the young children are all safe and other toys and equipment stored in places where adults can safely access them.
- Toys should be regularly checked for damage and wear making sure there are no sharp edges.

Further reading, information and sources

Ward, S. (2000) *Babytalk*. London: Century

Henderson, A. (1992) *Play and Learning for under-threes*. Pre-school Learning Alliance

Goldschmied E. and Jackson S. (1994) *People Under Three*. London: Routledge

Silberg, J. (1999) *Games to Play with Babies*. Dunstable Brilliant Publications

Babies and toddlers NVQ links

Level 2
C 8.1, C 9.1, C 9.5, P 1.2, C 13.3
Level 3
C 3.1, C 3.4, C 10.2, C 11.2, C 11.3, C 11.5, C 16, M 7, P 2.1, P 2.3, P 2.4, C 14.3, C 14.4, C 14.5

14

After School and Holiday Clubs

The National Curriculum prescribes the activities for children in the early years of the primary school. Programmes of study and attainment targets structure the planning framework. However, many children get the opportunity to undertake a wider range of open ended activities at after school or holiday clubs.

We have taken photographs of some of the 4 to 8 year old children at the Holiday Club which is run in our nursery school. The older children use the school resources augmented by some extra craft equipment, outdoor apparatus and computer software. The children are given the opportunity to choose from the workshop provision and organise their time. They decide what they want to do or make and can continue uninterrupted for long periods. Children with identified special educational needs are given extra support to ensure access to the full range of learning and play opportunities. Staff offer focus activities such as cooking, craft, organised games and puppets. They also introduce themes such as shadows, festival celebrations, dinosaurs, houses, holidays and use current film themes.

In this chapter we have given examples of a range of activities undertaken in the Holiday Club. The learning processes are illustrated through our descriptions of the activities and the responses of some of the children.

One important advantage of a mixed age range is the relaxed and informal way the children work and play together. All using their skills and abilities to work alongside or co-operate. Much is learned through watching and from interaction with each other. Children are able to negotiate and share resources and organise turn taking with equipment such as the computer. Children who attended the nursery school together but go to different primary schools often meet up again and renew friendships at the holiday club. It is gratifying for staff to see how mature and settled the children have become. Continuity in contact with local families helps to promote a sense of community and increases the effectiveness of the nursery.

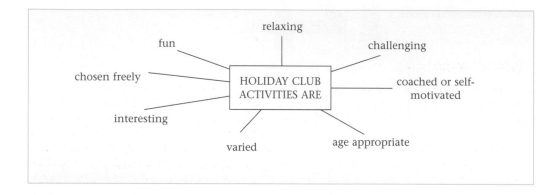

relaxing

fun

challenging

chosen freely

HOLIDAY CLUB
ACTIVITIES ARE

coached or self-
motivated

interesting

varied

age appropriate

CHAPTER FOURTEEN *Activity*

A sand hill for snakes

The shallow sand tray was available with a quantity of dry sand and a range of models of insets and mini beasts. This group of friends stayed with this activity over quite a long period and developed the story as they played together. They made mounds of sand and made different homes for the creatures. There was lots of discussion about the models and the animals they represented. At times they were absorbed by making patterns in the sand as they moved it around with their hands. At times they played imaginatively – 'it's an island', 'no it's a volcano'. At times they talked of other things and experiences. At times other children joined the play for short periods. The quality of concentration and involvement showed the value and relevance of providing a material such as sand and small world figures for older children as well as younger ones.

CHAPTER FOURTEEN *Activity*

Cooking mince pies

A member of staff supported this activity. She checked that children washed their hands well before starting and called them in the order they signed up on the waiting list for their turn. All the children were invited to cook a mince pie as a present to take home at the end of the session. Each child had their own bowl and mixing spoon. The recipe showed how many spoonsful of fat, flour and sugar to mix the pastry. They filled the pastry case with mince meat and wrote a name label before putting in the baking tray. The activity was relaxed as children talked about many topics as well as discussing the process of making the mince pies.

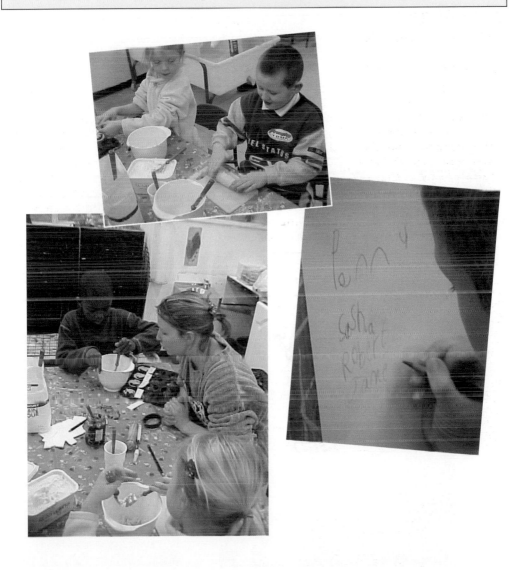

CHAPTER FOURTEEN *Activity*

Decorating a box or tin

This craft activity was offered if children wished to make something for themselves or as a Christmas present for their friends/family. The boxes and tins had been acquired from a scrap scheme and sheets and squares of shiny paper, scissors and pva glue in yoghurt pots and spatulas were on the table. Other tools, pens and papers were available from the nearby storage trolley in this graphics area. The children concentrated for long periods and were pleased with the end products. Each had very different ideas of what they wanted to achieve. Lucy and her friend Natasha choose a tin each and cut a hole in the lid to make money boxes. Lianna also chose this and enjoyed covering around the circular shape. Michaela covered her box carefully all in red while Cassie made a tessellated pattern with two colours. She later repeated this with two different colours on another side and took a bag of coloured squares home to complete the rest. April decided that her toy puppy needed a kennel. She chose to mount the shiny paper squares with larger backing squares of orange making a symmetrical pattern.

CHAPTER FOURTEEN *Activity*

Taking turns with a computer game

Three girls were waiting for a turn on the computer. They asked an adult who should go first. She asked who they thought should have first turn and refused to make the decision for them. So the two older children said Leah should go first as she was the youngest. The oldest girl, Bryony, then realised she would be last and there was further discussion. They did stick with this solution timing each turn with the sand timer to make sure it was fair. They all enjoyed watching and talking about the elements in the game.

CHAPTER FOURTEEN *Activity*

Painting together

Robert invited his younger brother James to do a painting with him at the easel. Each started painting an animal on separate halves of the sheet. They were absorbed in their own painting but made comments about each others work. Robert painted a giraffe and James a monster. James experimented by layering on more paint using brushes in both hands, while Robert painted a wiggley frame around their painting. Both boys were very pleased with their joint efforts and Robert signed both of their names. Again the provision of paint to be accessed at any time during the session is valued by older and younger children.

CHAPTER FOURTEEN *Activity*

Making a tube train tunnel

A range of scrap materials were provided in the technology area. A range of tools and joining materials were also available. Children used these independently and very actively. They chose what to use and what to make. Some made things to use in other areas of play such as walkie talkies and long ribbon material bands around their heads and waists. Stewart and Ruben attend the same primary school in different classes. Their construction was too big for the table so they took over the floor in the adjacent story room. The design work changed and evolved over the day. Although undertaking other activities, including outdoor play, the boys returned to this work. There was much discussion about the tunnel, the track and how to put the whole model together. The following day they got together again and made a three dimensional model using every cardboard tube in the school. This posed many more technical problems of joining and stability. Other children would come and watch and talk with them about their model.

CHAPTER FOURTEEN *Activity*

Parachute Games

At the end of the holiday club the furniture is pushed aside so that all the children and staff can join in together. First they played at lifting the parachute up high forming a mushroom shape allowing space for different groups of children to run underneath, for example all those wearing yellow or all those with laces in their shoes. Then they played games of cat and mouse where two children go under the parachute and two other children are chosen to be 'cats' and go on top and catch these 'mice'. All the others around the edges flip the parachute so the mice are hidden as they scurry about. The final activity involved four children sitting back to back in the very centre of the parachute. Everyone else walks around twisting the parachute around them, keeping it low so that it does not go near their faces. The person controlling the game says when to stop and counts to three when everyone walks backwards pulling the parachute hard outwards. The children in the middle are spun around. These games have involved the whole group in active participation and make a communal ending to the club. Parents and families arrive and watch at the end before saying goodbye.

Equal opportunities – access to the learning

with reference to the policy of the holiday club organisers and providers:

- The only admissions criteria is age and a waiting list system is in place – the provision is advertised in the locality and throughout Croydon in the summer.
- All children are able to choose from a whole range of activities in a workshop provision.
- Staff encourage older and younger children to play together and are especially aware of children who come from different schools,

ensuring all children are relaxed and involved.

- No child is turned away from an activity they choose – strategies for turn taking are supported.
- The booking form asks parents/carers to identify any special needs to enable staff to plan individual support and ensure all activities are accessible to all children.
- Staff state that they value the children's opinions and involve them in choosing role play activities.

Health and safety

with reference to the policies of the holiday club organisers and providers:

- All parents are made aware of the policies.
- All staff have knowledge of the policies and their duty to keep everyone safe.
- Staff ensure children go home with the parent/carer who brought them or other persons they nominate – any access difficulties are noted in confidence.
- The booking form asks parents/carers to state any allergies or medical conditions.
- Areas able to be accessed by the children to be clean, in safe working order,

equipment checked, only used for purpose designed and sited sensibly to allow safe movement of the children and staff.

- All materials to be non-toxic.
- Suitable footwear and clothing is to worn both by staff and children.
- In the outdoor area wheeled toys and climbing equipment are used safely in separate areas.
- Staff, children and adults to be aware of emergency procedures.
- Staff always cover outside sandpit to avoid soiling by animals such as cats and foxes.

After school and holiday clubs NVQ links

Early Years Care and Education
Level 2

C 1.2, C 4.2, C 4.5, C 8.1, C 8.3, C 8.4, E 1.1, E 2.1

Level 3

C 3, C 5.2, C 7.2, C 10, C 11.2, E 3.1, E 3.3, M7

Playwork
Level 2

PA 2.2, PA 3.1, PA 3.3, PA 3.4

Level 3

PB 23.1, PB 23.2, PB 23.3, PB 23.4, PC 12.2

Theorists, References and Reading

Early years practice has been informed and influenced by many pioneers such as Isaacs, McMillan, Montessori, Piaget, Vygotsky, Malaguzzi and Bruce. They have all developed theories and ways of working which have influenced practice and have been applied, modified and extended. Research in the settings and continuous reflection supports this process. Raising questions, observing and recording how children are learning and evaluating the practice to see what is effective in meeting the children's needs.

Jean Piaget (1896–1980) is probably the best known and most quoted theorist. He emphasised the interaction of the individual child and the environment, taking for granted any social relationships. He saw the child as active in using first hand and prior experiences in order to learn. Play helps the child to make sense of these experiences and come to terms with the world. Piaget outlined a development in a child's play from the sensory experiences of a baby through the pretend play of the pre-schooler to play using rules practiced by older children.

Maria Montessori (1870–1952) also saw the child as an active learner. Her work was carried out in Rome where, through much observation, she deduced that children reach sensitive stages of development when they are receptive to certain areas of learning. From this she developed a structured teaching programme using materials which encourage children to use their hands, progressing from a simple to a complex exercise, whilst working alone. Her methods are said to stifle creativity and, because there is little interaction with others, do not foster language development and social skills. Montessori did not see the value of play.

In contrast, Vygotsky in the Soviet Union and Bruner in the United States stressed the importance of the social and cultural context in children's learning. **Lev Vygotsky (1896–1935)** used the term 'zone of proximal development' (translation 1978) to describe the part played by either an adult or more knowledgeable peer in aiding a child. What a child can do with help now he will be able to do alone later. He saw play as enabling children to make sense of what they are learning without the limitations of real-life situations. Role play prepares them for such situations and through this a child functions at a higher level.

Jerome Bruner (1915–) felt that children learnt by 'doing' and that the learning was in three stages. In the first (enactive) stage the child needs to have first hand, direct experiences which are recalled in the second (iconic) stage through books, interest tables etc. The third (symbolic) stage includes the recording of these experiences through talking, drawing and writing. Adults are necessary to make the task more manageable for the child, they provide a scaffold. Routines and informal interactions are important for learning.

Like Bruner, **Friedrich Froebel (1782–1852)** stressed the importance of the child being physically active and having real experiences. He encouraged the expressive arts – music and movement, arts and crafts and finger rhymes – as well as a love of literature and mathematical understanding. These activities were to be carried out both indoors and outside. He believed that parents are the first educators of the child and that they should be welcomed into schools.

Margaret McMillan (1860–1931) was a follower of Froebel. Her work was in the United Kingdom where she set up nursery schools as an extension of home with a strong partnership with parents. She stressed the importance of good nourishment and health, pioneering school meals and medical services. First hand experience and active learning were also important to her, and she felt that relationships, feelings and ideas should be stressed.

Also influenced by Froebel, **Susan Isaacs (1885–1948)**, like McMillan, saw nurseries as an extension of home and stressed the importance of parents as the best educators of their children. Through observing children in Cambridge she saw the value of play which gives them the freedom to move in and out of reality and so achieve a balance in ideas, feelings and relationships.

Loris Malaguzzi, a recent educator, has made a significant contribution to early childhood learning with the development after the war of community schools in Reggio Emilia in Northern Italy. He describes the 'hundred languages of children', which include movement, sound, mark making, stories etc., through which parents and educators are encouraged to help children develop an understanding of their world. Like Froebel, Malaguzzi emphasised the use of children's bodies as well as their minds. Through exhibitions in this country the work of Reggio Emilia is having a great influence on current practice in British early years settings.

Tina Bruce, a present day early years specialist, uses the term 'free-flow play'. This involves the child indulging in his ideas, feelings and relationships whilst applying control and competence which have been gained from earlier experience. Bruce sees play as a starting point for other activities.

Further reading, information and sources

Bruce, T. (1996) *Helping Young Children To Play*. London: Hodder and Stoughton.

Edwards, C., Gandini, L. and Forman, G. (1995) *The Hundred Languages of Children*. New Jersey: Ablex Publishing.

Moyles, J. (1990) *Just Playing? – The Role and Status of Play in Early Childhood Education*. Buckingham: OU Press.

Pascal C. Bertram A. (1997) *Effective Early Learning*. London: Hodder and Stoughton.

Robson S. and Smedley S. (editors) (1996) *Education in Early Childhood – First Things First*. London: David Fulton Publishers Ltd.

Playing and Learning at Home. National Association of Toy and Leisure Libraries, 68 Church Way, London NW1 1LT. Tel: 020 7383 2714.

Vygotsky, L. (1978) *Mind in Society*. Cambridge, M.A Harvard University Press.

Biddulph. L. and McQueen, D. 'How to Help Talking, A Practical Handbook'. The Secretary, Speech and Language Department, Beecroft, Cannock Chase Hospital, Brunswick Road, Cannock, Staffordshire WS11 2XY.

DfEE/QCA *Early Learning Goals* 2000 QCA/00/587.

Various local authorities have published useful early years curriculum documents we have found those from Westminster and Lewisham especially valuable.

Reader's would find these two books complement their effective planning through observation and assessment and knowledge of the different ages and stages of child development:

Jackie Harding and Liz Meldon-Smith (2000) *How to Make Observations and Assessments* 2nd Edn. London: Hodder and Stoughton.

Jackie Harding and Liz Meldon-Smith (2000) *Helping Young Children to Develop* 2nd Edn. London: Hodder and Stoughton.

Pre-school Learning Alliance publications can be obtained from: Mailing House, 45–49 Union Road, Croydon, CR0 2XU. Tel: 0870 603 0062, Fax: 020 8684 0485.

Glossary

These are not dictionary definitions but the authors' understanding and use of the terms.

SCHEMA	Patterns of action or behaviour which link to the formation of concepts or mental maps- during the formation of these concepts children explore the ideas in many different learning situations for long periods repeating actions and adjusting them as their map develops, becomes more complex and extended. They are a useful way of adults looking at children's active learning. There are different classifications of schemas: Horizontal and Vertical Trajectory children – explore moving themselves and objects along these planes – older children develop an interest in grids Enclosing and Enveloping children make boundaries and form edges around themselves and objects. They often cover them or themselves up or put things inside each other (bags and boxes) hiding away Joining and Connecting – children physically link things together often using string, tape and other joiners. They enjoy train tracks and construction toys Rotational – children are interested in objects that go round such as wheels, whisks, cogs, turning taps and other objects.
PROBLEM SOLVING	Children experimenting and finding solutions they are satisfied with to practical problems.
BLOCKS	Large wooden bricks which are mathematically congruent. Sets made by Community Playthings consist of solid units of increasing size, shaped blocks and hollow blocks – both small and large.
SMALL WORLD	Representations of objects and people on a small scale. Children can manipulate and play various senarios.
ROLE PLAY	Acting out the different roles that adults take in the community or becoming a fantasy figure or animal. This empowers the children to experience what it might feel like to take on that role.

PRACTITIONER	Adults who work with children in early years settings often with a range of experience/qualifications.
EARLY YEARS	Children from 0–8 years of age.
EARLY YEARS SETTING	The range of provision where young children are cared for and educated outside their own homes e.g. All nursery schools; local authority, maintained, independent, private, voluntary; integrated centres; pre-schools; child minder networks.
ONSET	The sound of the first syllable or part of a word e.g. C- for cat, CH for church.
RIME	The rhyming last syllable or part of the word, e.g. at in cat sat mat.
ORDINAL	Numbers in sequence or order – first second third.
CARDINAL	Numbers which show quantity – one, two, five.
PELMANISM	Matching pairs – often played with cards face down and players turn over 2 cards and try to remember where their are matching pairs.
SYMBOLIC PLAY	To use an object or an action to stand in the place of the real thing – using a stick for a horse.
REPRESENTATIONAL PLAY	Making a mark or action to represent an object, event or emotion.
IMAGINATIVE PLAY	Developing ideas and sequences in fantasy rather than reality.
PEERS	People of a similar age in a community together.
SIBLINGS	Brothers and sisters.
DISPOSITION	A natural inclination towards a course of action which can be developed and extended.
NURTURING	To foster a sense of well being as a mother does with her baby, and the influence of the caring world around the child on their development.
DIFFERENTIATION	Practioners ensuring that learning opportunities are accessible by individual children with a range of abilities, dispositions, knowledge and skills.
LEUVEN SCALES	A scheme which enables a record to be made of the level of involvement of a child in an activity and an acknowledgement of the depth of their learning. Developed by Professor Laevers at the University of Leuven.
FOUND MATERIAL	Recycled packaging or other materials which may be discarded but which can be used creatively – need to ensure safety and cleanliness.
ACETATE	Flexible plastic film or sheets which may be coloured can be used for experiment.
CONSERVATION	Stage of mathematical thinking described by Jean Piaget when a child has experience with differing amounts of materials and their properties in different situations.
KINAESTHETIC	Sensation by which bodily position, weight, muscle tension and movement are perceived.